"As a woman of color, I've worked to ensure that diversity and inclusion have been cornerstones of our culture at Honest since our founding in 2012. Embracing each person's unique heritage, celebrating diversity, and ensuring inclusivity inspires us to be better teammates, leaders, parents, and friends. James White has been an invaluable resource here at Honest, and we're lucky to have his support and guidance as we continue to foster a truly equitable environment."

 —**JESSICA ALBA**, founder and Chief Creative Officer,
 the Honest Company

"What a refreshing read! When a CEO tells you (in print) that he has never been promoted based on his potential, and when his millennial daughter is partnering with her dad in real time in the real world, you have a tool that touches every part of your personal and professional life. *Anti-Racist Leadership* gives you the steps to get started and be successful in your endeavors in our next normal."

 —**JIM DONALD**, Cochair and former CEO, Albertsons;
 former CEO, Starbucks

"CEOs, please don't delegate the reading of this book. If you do, your organization will stay the same, and you'll be saying 'We have a long way to go.' If you read it and follow White's detailed blueprint, you'll be able to say 'Look how far we've come.'"

 —**MICHAEL C. BUSH**, CEO, Great Place to Work

"James and Krista White have successfully provided something that fills the void so often left for those seeking actionable guidance in driving real DEI change. *Anti-Racist Leadership* is a masterful blend of tangible examples, straightforward frameworks, and double-

and triple-clicks into the DEI 'why,' 'how to,' and 'what not to' checklists. It delivers an incredibly human, digestible, and relevant set of learning moments that should be required education for any leader or company serious about the personal and organizational transformation necessary to move beyond DEI rhetoric and good intent."

 —**DAMIEN HOOPER-CAMPBELL**, Chief Diversity Officer, Zoom Video Communications

"Anti-Racist Leadership is a powerful and thought-provoking read for every leader who cares about company culture and inclusive leadership. It is necessary reading for every business leader in America today."

 —**RON SHAICH**, founder and former Chairman and CEO, Panera Bread

"Anti-Racist Leadership is unique and a must-read because White provides specific, tactical advice that leaders can execute immediately to drive lasting change."

 —**SHERYL O'LOUGHLIN**, cofounder, J.E.D.I. (Justice, Equity, Diversity, and Inclusion) Collaborative; cofounder and Board Chair, Women on Boards Project; former CEO, REBBL and Clif Bar & Company; and cofounder and former CEO, Plum Organics

"This book provides a detailed road map for current and future leaders who want to consciously work on creating an anti-racist workplace and society. It challenges leaders to examine their practices and encourages them to create a space of belonging, where everyone can find their purpose and achieve success without fear of being ostracized. I will use it as a guide for my work as a nonprofit leader and for young leaders entering the workplace. Thank you, James

White, for providing the first introspective leadership book by a Black leader who made it to the top. You are a hero and a leader for so many!"

—**CHERYL L. JONES**, President and CEO, Girls Inc. of St. Louis

"Transformation of growing businesses is a by-product of clarity of purpose, building processes that enable positive momentum, and holding leaders accountable. I've been waiting for years for James D. White to share his insights on how to build growth businesses by incorporating diversity, equity, and inclusion within the culture. The time has come."

—**MICHAEL C. HYTER**, President and CEO, the Executive Leadership Council

"The book is indeed provocative, but that's precisely what's needed as we look to advance the biggest growth opportunity in a generation. The counsel James White provides in this book draws on his lived experiences. He demonstrates how business leaders can create pathways and opportunities for more diverse leadership, a major milestone on the journey to a more inclusive and stronger economy. He offers comprehensive advice for corporate executives looking to get serious about creating an equitable and anti-racist company culture."

—**DARYL BREWSTER**, CEO, Chief Executives for Corporate Purpose (CECP)

"I encourage everyone to read *Anti-Racist Leadership*, written by our very own Board Chair, James D. White. This important book will help leaders build a truly equitable work environment. All of us at Honest are lucky to learn from James and have his support and guidance as we continue to foster a truly diverse and inclusive environment, every day."

—**NICK VLAHOS**, CEO, the Honest Company

"In a world where we need to drive real change in DEI practices in every company and at every level, all leaders need this book in order to learn how to eliminate racism—overt, subtle, and systemic. James White's executive skills and integrity have always stood out, and *Anti-Racist Leadership* is the first practical guide written by someone who has lived both the experience of feeling racism and the experience of removing it. There is so much to do, and this is a marvelous addition to the lexicon on DEI for everyone."

—**BRACKEN P. DARRELL**, President and CEO, Logitech International

"Replete with concrete examples from his own experience as a CEO and that of many other leaders, White's book should be read and absorbed by anyone serious about making real progress on diversity and inclusion."

—**JOAN C. WILLIAMS**, Distinguished Professor of Law and founding Director, Center for WorkLife Law, UC Hastings Law

Anti-Racist Leadership

Anti-Racist Leadership

HOW TO TRANSFORM CORPORATE CULTURE IN A RACE-CONSCIOUS WORLD

James D. White
with Krista White

HARVARD BUSINESS REVIEW PRESS
BOSTON, MASSACHUSETTS

The web addresses referenced in this book were live and correct at the time of the book's publication but may be subject to change.

Library of Congress Cataloging-in-Publication Data

Names: White, James D., 1960– author.
Title: Anti-racist leadership : how to transform corporate culture in a
    race-conscious world / James D. White.
Description: Boston, MA : Harvard Business Review Press, [2022] | Includes
    index.
Identifiers: LCCN 2021043261 (print) | LCCN 2021043262 (ebook) |
    ISBN 9781647821975 (hardcover) | ISBN 9781647821982 (ebook)
Subjects: LCSH: Anti-racism. | Leadership. | Corporate culture. |
    Executives. | Social responsibility of business.
Classification: LCC HT1563 .W48 2022 (print) | LCC HT1563 (ebook) |
    DDC 305.8—dc23/eng/20211109
LC record available at https://lccn.loc.gov/2021043261
LC ebook record available at https://lccn.loc.gov/2021043262

ISBN: 978-1-64782-197-5
eISBN: 978-1-64782-198-2

The paper used in this publication meets the requirements of the American National Standard for Permanence of Paper for Publications and Documents in Libraries and Archives Z39.48-1992.

To my beautiful daughter Krista—your thoughtful spirit and tenacity to create more inclusive spaces in the world was my inspiration for this project. Your forceful and kind voice for real change, insightful questions around the status quo, and unwavering hopefulness that we can all be better leaders has been an inspiration and a blessing. Forever grateful, Dad.

Contents

Introduction: Why All Business Leaders Must Be   1
Anti-Racist Leaders

1. Intentional Leadership Matters   7

2. CEO-Driven Change   35

3. How to Begin   63

4. Transforming the Culture by Design   95

5. Building Inclusive Leadership into the   125
   Company DNA

6. Building an Inclusive Ecosystem   147

7. Culture Is the Key That Unlocks the Future,   169
   and the Future Is Now

Appendix: Resources for Further Learning   195

Notes   203
Index   211
Acknowledgments   221
About the Authors   223

Anti-Racist Leadership

Why All Business Leaders Must Be Anti-Racist Leaders

This book is not apolitical. This book is explicitly anti-racist, pro-Black, pro-LGBTQIA+, and feminist. This book takes the stance that Black Lives Matter, that LGBTQIA+ rights are human rights, that people of all abilities deserve respect and access, and that people of all genders have the right to sovereignty over their bodies and identities. This book acknowledges that capitalism is built on a foundation of systemic racism and that to have a truly diverse, equitable, and inclusive work environment we must acknowledge the historic and present injustices faced by marginalized people.

Through my thirty-plus years of experience as an operating executive, I have made diversity, equity, and inclusion (DEI) driving forces in my leadership vision. I have seen the impact of culture on organizations at every level, from startup to *Fortune* 500, and in both private and public companies.

Through my lived experiences as a Black man in the highest levels of corporate America, and from listening to my two outspoken millennial daughters, I have learned that the time is past due to take more-direct action in the fight for social justice. Often, doing the right thing is not the easy thing. To create truly inclusive cultures in the corporate world—which is now a necessity for all forward-thinking businesses—we must take on an entire system built on inequality.

Business leaders hold an important position in the power structure of our country, and they have the unique ability to reach thousands of employees and millions of consumers with their leadership. Building anti-racist companies by design makes for great places to work for *all*.

One of the most consistent challenges I've seen CEOs face is how to use organizational culture and people strategies to drive better results. Executives across the board know they should care about diversity, equity, and inclusion. So why are so few getting it right?

Part of the answer lies in a society that has not provided equal opportunities to all, combined with a corporate world in which managers tend to recruit and hire the people who come from privilege because they're the ones who seem like the best "cultural fit." The result is generations of business leaders who don't even know where to find people from different backgrounds. But our country's demographics are changing rapidly. The smartest business leaders know that they must access the best and brightest talent, with the best ideas for meeting the needs of a changing world, a world where anti-racist leadership isn't just an option but a necessity for a thriving business.

To those who might still wonder if DEI is a zero-sum game that penalizes the straight white men who were for so long the *only* people who fit the corporate culture, know that anti-racism leadership is about creating more opportunities for all. Anti-racism challenges *all* of us to be the best business leaders we can be.

Written during the Covid-19 pandemic and the revival of the Black Lives Matter movement, *Anti-Racist Leadership* has been a labor of love. It was one of the things that kept me energized during an exceedingly difficult time in our collective history. As the pandemic threw inequity into greater extremes, I knew this book was more necessary than ever. The pandemic tested leaders in ways they wouldn't previously have thought possible, and it exposed the dark reality of business rooted in exploitation and oppression. This time, DEI was life and death. When employees aren't provided with the proper protections that should have been afforded to them as human beings, the results are dire. Whether because of nefariousness or unchecked bias, businesses by and large treated the mainly Black and brown working-class frontline staff at grocery stores, delivery services, and other essential businesses as disposable. Our response to Covid-19 was unacceptable. We must do better by our fellow humans. And it starts at the top.

One of the highlights of writing this book was the opportunity to work with my eldest daughter, Krista, a writer and actor in New York City. We are building a company together called Culture Design Lab, through which we'll work with boards and CEOs to transform organizational cultures.

Krista pushed me to be more radical with my message. "Dad, you're taking on a system that was built on discrimination," she warned me early on. I knew from experience that she was right—after all,

I've lived through many challenges as a Black leader over the past thirty years. But while I have always been a passionate champion of diversity, I am also a mainstream corporate executive.

Then came the racially charged incidents that left Breonna Taylor, Ahmaud Arbery, George Floyd, Rayshard Brooks, Tony McDade, and other Black Americans dead, and the Black Lives Matter demonstrations that followed. Racism was the same as it had always been in America, but for the corporate world, the blinders fell in the spring and summer of 2020. Any number of white business leaders began contacting me asking if I could advise them on what they could do to be part of the solution. I knew I had a role to play in ridding corporate America of the racism that is always detrimental and sometimes fatal to so many members of our society.

I am grateful to Krista for her voice and passion, which deeply influenced the direction we took in this book. My daughter helped me see how important it was that we take a stand on the right side of history, letting our voices ring loud and true as Black folks. We, too, sing America.

Anti-Racist Leadership is part memoir and part practical field guide for CEOs and other leaders who are looking to transform their company culture to suit the needs of a new decade. This book is for you if you are:

- a C-suite executive or board member creating, or wanting to start creating, structural change at your organization

- an HR director passionate about improving company culture

- the head of a DEI program working to operationalize your agenda

- a senior manager who wants to level-up your leadership skills

- an emerging leader preparing yourself and your business for the transformations of tomorrow

In the chapters that follow, I will present the concrete steps all business leaders today should take to mend a broken system. By the end, you'll be ready to be part of the solution, with a tangible plan for preparing your organization to tackle the needs of our increasingly multicultural world.

To the people who pick this up who are in a position of power or privilege, read this book with an open heart.

And to the young people, the LGBTQIA+ folks, the Black and Asian and Indigenous and Latinx people, the people with disabilities, and anyone existing in any marginalized identity or intersection, let's go out there and change the world.

1

Intentional Leadership Matters

I t was late May 2020, a time when people of every color were
defying the Covid-19 pandemic to take to the streets to show
their outrage. On Memorial Day, May 25, in Minneapolis,
seventeen-year-old Darnella Frazier used her smartphone to capture
a full video of police officer Derek Chauvin kneeling on George Floyd's
neck for nine minutes, until Floyd died, after he'd been stopped on
suspicion of using a counterfeit $20 bill to buy cigarettes. It was only
the latest in thousands of similar incidents throughout history—but
this time change was brewing, even in the corporate world.

I could tell that something was different by the sheer volume of calls
and emails I was getting from business leaders expressing a wish to
do something about racism and police violence.

At that point, the global economy was on the verge of collapse from
the pandemic, and I had already started working on a book about how
to create the kind of diverse, inclusive organizational culture that

would make every business more resilient whether times are good or bad. However, after the George Floyd tragedy and the new wave of Black Lives Matter demonstrations—from Portland to Paris—I realized that the corporate world, along with the entire nation, needed to do a lot of soul searching in order to make those cultural changes. There are deep-rooted reasons behind corporate America's failure to be fully inclusive.

I am a Black executive who has been transforming corporate cultures to make them more intentionally inclusive throughout my career, a career that officially began when I joined Coca-Cola in 1983, right after college, and that continued through—and beyond—my time as CEO at Jamba Juice, from 2008 to 2016, where my main mission was to turn around a company that was losing money and fighting for survival. In my time at Jamba Juice, I tripled the diversity at the top three levels and increased the diversity of the top two levels from 20 percent to 50 percent—meaning that our executive teams included people of color, women, members of the LGBTQIA+ community, and even white males who didn't fit the usual profile of a "cultural fit." (I've worked with some brilliant white males who have needed someone to recognize their potential, in some cases because they were older, in others because they hadn't gone to the "right" schools or come from the "right" socioeconomic lineage.) Over that same period the company's market cap soared 500 percent. This is not a coincidence. When you have a corporate culture of true meritocracy, empowering your entire workforce to bring its talents and problem-solving skills to the table, the results are better than when only some people can.

Countless studies have backed this premise. To mention just two, *The Wall Street Journal*'s first corporate ranking of diversity, equity, and inclusion (DEI) among S&P 500 companies, in late 2019, found a direct link between DEI and a competitive edge, while a Boston Consulting Group study found that companies with above-average diversity on their management teams also reported innovation revenue that was 19 percentage points higher than that of companies with below-average leadership diversity—45 percent of total revenue versus just 26 percent.[1] If anything, DEI will be even more important in the future. As my daughters keep reminding me, millennials and Generation Z—the consumer and investor base of the 2020s and beyond—embrace multiculturalism and LGBTQIA+ identity. The young generations consider the intentional values of the companies they do business with and the brands they buy.

Why, when we've been confronted over and over with proof that DEI is great for business, have leaders resisted instituting the changes that make a company truly diverse and inclusive?

A number of factors might get in the way. First, not everyone actually understands what DEI looks like. I've seen CEOs issue statements that say, "We support diversity." That isn't enough; you have to live it. Nor is it enough just to bring one woman and one person of color onto the board and into the C-suite and rely on meritocracy to take care of the rest. You need to be intentional in building a pipeline of diverse individuals to be tomorrow's leaders.

Second, achieving true DEI is hard. It requires a new approach to everything from recruiting to assignments to determining what makes someone a "fit" in the organization. Achieving DEI takes time—in most companies several years of highly intentional changes, all driven by the CEO. It takes leadership, committed to creating a diverse, anti-racist culture that is integrated into every aspect of the business, including the supply chain and the overall ecosystem. It takes applying analytics, priorities, and goals with the same rigor that a top executive uses to ensure success in every other area of the business.

However, these days more business leaders than ever before are asking how to make their organizations diverse, inclusive, and anti-racist. McKinsey found that in the year after George Floyd's murder, companies across the United States committed approximately $200 billion to racial-justice efforts.[2] Moreover, diversity is a demographic fact, and to drive innovation in this diverse world we need diverse talent. Inclusiveness isn't simply nice to have; *not* being inclusive will lead to failure.

The Time for Change Is Now

I'm now an advisor to a few startups run by people of color, and I sit on the boards of some very progressive companies (including Adtalem Global Education and Medallia, the latter of which makes customer-experience software) as well as on those of several nonprofits aimed at helping businesses achieve a positive societal impact. In addition, I cofounded an organization called the Directors Academy, which seeks to identify, develop, and advance the next generation of diverse corporate board members. My presence as a Black business leader on a board speaks for a certain amount of diversity, but in addition, I've been highly outspoken about what companies need to do when it comes to cultural transformation. So it is not surprising that in the weeks following the George Floyd killing, I received at least a dozen calls and emails from board members, CEOs, and investors wanting to talk about the moment and the need for change.

Among those I heard from was a venture-capitalist friend who told me that her fourteen-year-old son found the George Floyd video online and was horrified. "You can't look away," she told me, "when your fourteen-year-old asks, 'Mom, why do we live in a world like this?'" Especially when her son seemed to be implying that he had additional questions, such as "What are you and Dad doing about this?" and "How could you let this happen?"

A former colleague from my years at Gillette who is now the CEO of a large distribution company, one with fifteen thousand employees, told me he was well aware that many of his frontline workers were people of color while few in management were. "I want to figure out how to do this right and make material changes," he said. A friend who specializes in CEO and director recruitment at a large executive search firm told me he thinks many executives now understand why the Black Lives Matter movement is so important, but we're still up against a major barrier in the corporate world.

"Amy Cooper is everywhere, at least metaphorically," my executive-recruiter friend said, referring to the former Franklin Templeton portfolio manager who, in another headline-grabbing May 2020 incident, called the police when she had an argument in Central Park with Christian Cooper (the two are not related), a Black man who was bird-watching and who asked her to leash her dog, as is required by law. What was especially revealing was the way Ms. Cooper told the police, in a hysterical tone, that an African American man was threatening her—which he wasn't. She has been seen as having leaned on her white privilege, weaponizing the police against a man who had simply asked her to comply with the park rules.

Ms. Cooper was fired from her job and charged with filing a false report—a charge that was later dismissed after she completed a series of restorative-justice sessions. But my friend made a point that I found chilling: think of what would have happened if she hadn't become the face of systemic racism. This presumably sophisticated Manhattanite, a financial-services executive with an MBA from the University of Chicago, might have gone through her whole career wielding racist assumptions and microaggressions in the workplace any time she had a role in selecting people for assignments, promotions, and interviews. For the most part, those biases might have been unconscious, blind spots that come from a lifetime of seeing the world through a lens of privilege, and all the more deadly because they were unspoken. She would have been in a position to hold people back because, as she saw it, their performance didn't cut it, or they didn't fit in.

I had to agree. I've seen Amy Coopers, metaphorically speaking, in the boardroom, the C-suite, and throughout the corporate hierarchy.

John Rice, the founder and CEO of the nonprofit Management Leadership for Tomorrow (MLT), one of the organizations that is at the forefront of developing leaders of color for the business world, calls this unspoken, often unconscious racism "third-degree racism."[3] He compares it to involuntary manslaughter: "We are not trying to hurt anyone, but we create the conditions that shatter somebody else's future aspirations." And actually, unacknowledged racism *was* fatal when the Covid-19 pandemic hit. Rice points to the Centers for Disease Control and Prevention mandate in the first few months of the pandemic that in order to get tested, you had to go to a primary-care doctor to get an order for the test and then, in some areas, also get a referral to a specialist who could approve a test. Many people of color do not have primary-care physicians. "If the people who designed that process knew up front that they would be exposed as racist, fired, and ostracized if their approach put minorities at a greater health risk than white people, they would have designed it differently and saved Black lives," Rice writes.

Now more than ever, we need senior executives who want to be intentional, inclusive, for-all leaders. These are terms I'll use throughout this book as I talk about leaders who are part of the solution to combatting systemic racism, leaders who place themselves squarely in the camp that says business leaders should be a force in the betterment of society, as opposed to following the Milton Friedman doctrine that the only social responsibility of business is to increase profits for its shareholders. To my mind there has never been a debate. As many of our other institutions are failing, CEOs have a responsibility not just to shareholders but to their broad set of stakeholders. Anti-racism should be easy; it's a matter of right and wrong.

Brian Cornell, the chairman and CEO of Target, which is based in Minneapolis, has been a shining example of this kind of intentional business leader. In 2020, following the Black Lives Matter demonstrations in his city, he announced a $10 million commitment to advance social justice and support rebuilding and recovery efforts in local communities, as well as an internal task force composed of senior leaders from across the company to keep working at creating change. Under his leadership Target has also committed $2 billion to support Black-owned businesses and launched a scholarship program for students attending historically Black colleges and universities.

None of this came as a surprise to me. I worked with Cornell when I was at Safeway, between 2005 and 2008. He was the chief marketing officer, and he recognized, well before most executives did, how diverse the customer base was and therefore how important it was to have a more inclusive management team that could tap into better market insights.

Another former colleague who has instilled a culture of caring wherever he goes is Bracken Darrell, the CEO of the tech accessory company Logitech. Following the murder of George Floyd, Darrell wrote in a piece posted on LinkedIn: "I am sorry. I hope you are, too. But sorry is not enough. We are all in this together. Equality and inclusion are incredibly important to me and the company that I run, Logitech. They are part of my values and our values, part of who we are."[4]

One CEO I didn't know who recognized the importance of speaking out was John Foley, the founder and CEO of the exercise-equipment maker Peloton. I received an email from his office because my wife and I own a Peloton stationary bicycle—and when I opened the email I saw an impressive message. Foley offered apologies for being "late to engaging directly with you on this—we have stood too quietly in the face of clear injustice. That ends today." Then he made a promise that "what's become clear to me is we must ensure this is an anti-racist organization. We should not be satisfied with ourselves unless we are intentionally and proactively changing our ways of thinking on a daily basis. We should not be satisfied with ourselves unless we are consistently tearing down the prejudices that facilitate such acts of hatred. And we should not be satisfied with ourselves until we are together dismantling the systemic structures that allow inequality to remain a fixture in our society." Since then, the company has made a pledge to dedicate $20 million to community investments and nonprofit partnerships fighting racial injustice.

It has been gratifying to see these financial commitments, because messages are just a gesture until you follow up with actions. The pages that follow provide concerned business leaders with a plan for taking action, and the reasons that they must.

One important reason is that the racist incidents of 2020 will continue to be repeated if people with a high-profile platform and a strong ability to influence—that's business leaders—don't acknowledge that there's a deep-rooted problem. After the murders of George Floyd et al., I had a horrendous sense of déjà vu. Just six years before, protests had broken out in Ferguson, Missouri, near my hometown of St. Louis, after police officer Darren Wilson shot Michael Brown, an unarmed Black teenager, and the nationwide Black Lives Matter movement had taken off.

In 2015 there had been massive student protests against racism at the University of Missouri (MU), my alma mater. The football team boycotted its own game against Brigham Young University, a move that cost MU $1 million, and Jonathan Butler, then a twenty-five-year-old graduate student, went on a hunger strike. Ultimately the protests led to both the president and the chancellor being fired for their lack of empathy. Students took note of what was going on, and enrollment declined by 35 percent between 2015 and 2017. When my good friend Alexander Cartwright (now the president at Central Florida University) was brought in as MU's chancellor at the start of the 2017 fall term, the board of trustees told him they needed to resolve what they defined as a "communication problem." No, it wasn't a communication problem; the school's reputation and coffers were suffering from documented cases of indifference to racial tensions.[5]

Little was resolved in 2014 and 2015, so new racist incidents were inevitable. This moment is different, though, and requires action. Business leaders who understand the moment and get it right stand to establish a strong competitive edge, for many reasons.

DEI Leads to Resilience

When I talk about a culture of diversity and inclusion, I don't just mean inclusion based on gender, ethnicity, and sexual orientation. While this kind of diversity is critical, it won't in itself have the kind of impact that a truly comprehensive view of DEI will. This threefold concept means valuing all aspects of identity (diversity); ensuring fair treatment and opportunity for all, with an effort to eliminate barriers that have kept some groups from realizing their full potential (equity); and bringing traditionally excluded people into decision-making processes and other roles that open doors to greater opportunities (inclusion). When I put DEI into practice, it means that we innovate and solve problems by looking at the issues from multiple perspectives. That can mean bringing experts in a variety of professional disciplines into the room, as well as a variety of socioeconomic and educational backgrounds, ages, religions, physical abilities, and views of the world. A truly inclusive corporate culture is one that accommodates all of the ways in which we are different from one another—and does so intentionally.

This kind of culture is indispensable to the corporation of the future, and to society at large. If you don't believe it, just consider what the consequences can be when there is no diversity at all in the room. When a certain political leader decided there wasn't going to be a pandemic in the United States, and shut down the voices of anyone who disagreed, including physicians and medical researchers who were infectious-disease specialists, the consequently delayed preventive measures against Covid-19 exacerbated an American death toll that is now in excess of 700,000 lives. In a crisis, you need to gather the best minds out there, and look at the problem from every conceivable angle in order to solve it.

In the current global downturn, some corporate managers and directors might be tempted to double down on the way things used to be. That is what appears to have happened after the financial crisis of 2008–2009, when many Wall Street firms were accused of laying off women in droves while retaining less qualified male employees. When companies have to become leaner, meaner operations, management might cut back on DEI for a number of reasons. Partly it's just because the lower-level jobs that management tends to see as disposable are where you'll find most of the women and people of color. But also, executives might find it easier to operate with everyone in agreement, with a vision focused on the singular goal of financial recovery. This, however, is extreme tunnel vision. During the pandemic, Didier Elzinga, the CEO of Culture Amp, held an international Zoom conference with a group of about twenty CEOs, in which he talked about how the crisis was likely to affect companies differently based on their corporate culture and on what kind of behavior they rewarded. "If you're a culture of 'eat what you kill' versus 'we hunt as a pack,' in the Covid-19 environment you're going to show up dramatically differently," he said. In the first culture, individual performance is everything. In the second, everyone benefits from the company's success.

McKinsey describes these two perspectives similarly, but uses the terms *efficiency* versus *resilience* in a report that says many business choices over the past decades traded resilience for a perceived increase in shareholder value. "Now may be the moment to consider that the era of chipping away at organizational resilience in the name of greater efficiency may have reached its limits," the report says. "This is not to say that there are no efficiencies to be sought or found, but more that the trade-off between efficiency and resiliency needs to be defined far more clearly than it has been in recent years."[6]

I see these appraisals as a call for a bold long-term vision. Such a vision should be aimed at ensuring that your company is resilient enough to weather a global economy that is full of uncertainties, and combining that with a focus on innovating for the future rather than just being cost-efficient now. Along with that kind of vision, this is a call for a corporate culture that gives everyone an incentive to be their best—because companies today need inspired teams that will work together to succeed in the post-Covid world.

But what about the countless corporations that have non-inclusive cultures and still succeed? It's true that for years companies have been able to excel financially without much attention to such cultural facets as human-rights records or even, in some cases, great customer relations. It's also true that all-white, all-male boards of many *Fortune* 500 companies have been able to generate megaprofits for their shareholders. But the same could be said of other business models that eventually failed to adapt to what was ahead. Sticking with a "this is what's always worked" attitude leads businesses to take their place in the scrapheap of once-prominent purveyors of floppy disks, video rentals, coal, and—well, you get the idea.

A Citigroup study from 2020 finds, in fact, that discrimination has already cost us significant business and economic growth. Citigroup estimates that between 2000 and 2020, the US gross domestic product lost $16 trillion as a result of discriminatory practices in a number of areas, including education and access to business loans. The study also finds that alleviating discrimination in these areas could add a $5 trillion boost to the economy over a five-year period.[7]

An earlier McKinsey study estimates that if the United States were to close the wealth gap that exists between black families and white families, we could add $1 trillion to $1.5 trillion to the country's economy—a GDP increase of between 4 percent and 6 percent—by 2028.[8]

Indeed, the capitalist system itself is under a lot of scrutiny now because it has left so many behind—and here we have two of the largest institutions serving the world's largest corporations presenting evidence that ending discrimination will be highly beneficial to the long-term health of the US economy. Capitalism is often treated as a game that rewards those who have the most opportunities, while they, in turn, through job creation and spending, create opportunities for others. The reality is more complicated; a rising tide *can* lift all boats, but first you have to make sure everyone has a boat and is not barred by discriminatory practices from taking it into the water.

The pandemic brought us some devastating reminders of how important it is for a CEO to build a corporate culture that doesn't leave anyone out. Take the meatpacking industry, which was well prepared for disease outbreaks that would threaten livestock but had no emergency plans in place for its own workforce. Most meatpacking companies resisted spacing their frontline workers apart, on the grounds that they needed to make every square inch of space efficient. There's no guessing what those frontline workers looked like; they were mostly Black and brown people, and the message was clear that their lives and health were expendable. A culture that prioritized keeping its production lines moving ultimately cost the industry in plant closures, not to mention a Covid-19 rate that, at the peak of the pandemic, reached nearly five hundred cases per 100,000 people per day, more than ten times the rate elsewhere in rural America.

In my years of transforming business cultures, I've seen that while business leaders often think of culture as secondary in importance to business goals, in reality you can't achieve those goals without a culture that creates a foundation for bringing out the best in everyone throughout the organization. You might say my experience is living proof of Harvard Business School professor and management guru Rosabeth Moss Kanter's theory of change management, which holds that the power structure itself is what drives behavior in an organization. An intentional leader gives everyone in the organization the room to innovate and think ahead.

Diversity, after all, is what sustains life on the whole planet. That's the conclusion of the Justice, Equity, Diversity, Inclusion (J.E.D.I.) Collaborative, an organization committed to diversity in the natural-foods industry. The founders are four women who've brought together their combined expertise in natural products, sustainability, and social justice—Lara Dickinson, MaryAnne Howland, Carlotta Mast, and Sheryl O'Loughlin. Part of what inspired them to start J.E.D.I. was the realization that human DEI is not so different from biodiversity all over. If the natural world is healthier when it has a greater level of biodiversity, why wouldn't our company environments be the same? The richer a company's diversity, and the stronger a company's commitment to creating a great experience for everyone, the greater the likelihood that *all* employees will do their best work.

How do you square DEI with the need to hire whoever seems to be the most qualified and capable candidate for the job? That's actually the wrong question to ask. It is misguided to view merit and diversity as opposing choices; it's a false choice because your hiring policy was never merit-based if you excluded significant portions of the population from the consideration set.

Frank Slootman, the CEO of the cloud database company Snowflake, inadvertently brought the fallacies of this argument to the business world's attention in June 2021, when he told Bloomberg TV that diversity should be secondary to merit in hiring. His comments set off a storm of criticism, and a week later Slootman walked back his words, telling *Silicon Valley Business Journal*: "Comments I made during a media interview . . . may have led some to infer that I believe that diversity and merit are mutually exclusive when it comes to recruitment, hiring, and promotion. I do not believe this, and I want to personally apologize to anyone who may have been hurt or offended by my comments."[9]

I don't mean that anyone should take the stance that "I see only a person's capabilities, not their color." I run when I hear that, actually. It means you don't appreciate my individual uniqueness as a Black man. A bad culture requires that everyone be a fit. A great culture, on the other hand, seeks cultural enhancements; not asking "How would this person fit in with us?" but "How would they enhance our culture?" The idea is that you make a deliberate effort to bring people with a wide range of lived experiences to the table.

For all of these reasons, it is critical now for business leaders to take an anti-racist, pro-Black, pro-LGBTQIA+, and feminist stand. Take a stand and then put those principles into practice, which means that you don't fall back on the old excuse that you can't find enough quali-fied people from underrepresented groups. Instead, you change your recruiting tactics, and you develop an internal pipeline of people who are developing skills that will qualify them for senior man-agement positions. It means that you seek diversity in your entire supply chain—the lawyers, accountants, bankers, and contractors you retain. It means you have a diverse board of directors who will bring perspectives no one previously considered to management decisions. It means you spend a lot of time listening to others.

Transformation Starts at the Top

In the summer of 2019, Krista and I attended Culture Amp's second annual Culture First conference in San Francisco. We were surrounded by an inspiring—and a diverse—crowd of attendees. But one crucial element was lacking; a large number of those in attendance were with-out board or CEO experience. Many came from HR and People Ops. They were very smart, but they didn't have the power to transform their corporate cultures.

The first rule of cultural transformation is that it absolutely, unequiv-ocally has to start at the top—from the CEO, with board support. HR and middle management simply cannot operationalize culture without the leadership and backing of senior management, and it's an uphill battle to relay the information that's needed to your CEO secondhand.

CEOs set a tone, and if CEOs demonstrate inclusive behavior in their actions and daily encounters, others will understand that this is the way things are done here. Culture sets the boundaries for what's possible, what's important, and what the company values. The CEO needs to create what I call the "burning platform"—the compelling reason for the organization and its people to want to change, clarifying not just the benefits and the risks of changing but also what will happen if change isn't achieved. The systems scientist Peter Senge calls organizations "invisible fabrics of interrelated actions."[10] It takes the CEO to create a culture that pervades all systems.

Sometimes it takes a CEO with the courage Todd Schnuck displayed in the wake of the Black Lives Matter demonstrations. He's the chairman and CEO of Schnuck Markets, a grocery-store chain that his grandmother founded in my hometown of St. Louis, and I serve on the company's board. Schnuck has embarked on a bold program whereby the company will stand for diversity no matter what the consequences. It started with listening tours around the company, and what he calls "courageous conversations" with local religious and community leaders who can talk to company executives about what it's like to be Black in St. Louis. In February 2021, Schnuck Markets observed Black History Month by posting a note for customers at the register, inviting them to round up their purchase to the nearest dollar and donate the change to an Urban League program called Save Our Sons, which helps young Black men enter the workforce. It's part of a charitable donation program the stores offer year-round, with recipient organizations that vary throughout the year.

This time, at a store in southeastern Missouri, an area that, as it happens, was part of my original sales territory when I was working for Coca-Cola, a white male customer looked at the sign and said to the checkout clerk, a Black woman, "Why does Schnuck keep trying to help the Negroes?"

"It was a very tough experience for the checker," says Schnuck. What the encounter revealed was not whether he should cater to racist customers, but that he should keep battling racism—and that's just what he's doing.[11]

An intentional leader also seeks out diverse talent. That requires seeing the potential in people and giving them the chance to develop leadership skills through assignments, training, mentorship, and sponsors within the company.

I know how important that is because I learned early on that at each step of my career, I was going to have to develop the skills I'd need for the next rung *before* I could be promoted. As an African American man, I've never been promoted based on my potential. What that means is, no one has ever said to me: "James, you did such a great job on the XYZ assignment that we're going to make you the head of our operations in China. You haven't had these responsibilities before, but we're going to promote you because we know you have the potential to grow into this role."

Yet in almost any organization, you'll find white males who are promoted to middle management, and then senior management, and then the C-suite, based on someone in the hierarchy determining that this young man has plenty of potential to become adept at the job. In this case *potential* can be code for the fact that the young man has degrees from the right schools, or that he came to the company highly recommended by the right people, or that he was born into the right family. Maybe his grandfather just happened to have been the founder of the company.

HR executives use the term "high potential"—or HiPo—when identifying employees who readily stand out for such qualities as talent, initiative, and cultural fit. Consulting firms might warn you that senior-management instinct or ad hoc observations are not enough to identify a HiPo, and there are metrics for determining potential through personality traits, but I believe it takes something more to judge a person's potential, particularly in a world where unconscious bias has held so many people back. We need to unravel that system. You might say that I, as a Black man, start from zero and have to gain points to prove why I'm there, while white male executives start from 100 and have to lose points to prove they *shouldn't* move on to greater responsibilities.

This kind of bias in favor of men who look completely "right" begins at hiring and then determines who gets access to the most important assignments, who gets mentors and sponsors, and who gets good performance evaluations—culminating in who gets promotions and higher compensation.

Conversely, if you view people through a biased lens and put them in a box labeled "wrong," you're dooming them to underperform. Not only do they miss the chance to gain the experience that proves what they're capable of doing, but they also might not stand out because they're putting most of their energy into protecting themselves against bias.

Catalyst, the sixty-year-old nonprofit organization that works with business leaders to build more-diverse workplaces, has found that when Asian, Black, Latinx, and multiracial employees in the United States and Canada feel they must be on guard at work to protect themselves against bias they pay an "emotional tax" that reduces their sense of psychological safety—and, unsurprisingly, diminishes their ability to contribute at work.

Michael C. Bush, the CEO of the workplace-culture consulting firm Great Place to Work, has led studies of how businesses lose out when marginalized employees don't feel psychologically safe. For example, a recent study found that at the average workplace, only 48 percent of LGBTQIA+ employees say their workplace is psychologically safe. The study then measured the impact on innovation and found that innovation decreases by a factor of three when white LGBTQIA+ employees don't feel psychologically safe, and by a factor of five for African American/Black, Asian, and Hispanic/Latino LGBTQIA+ employees in a similar environment.

An intentional leader makes sure that no coworkers are overlooked or underperforming because bias is putting them on the defensive. An intentional leader scopes out people who have the potential to grow into roles with more responsibility, looking past the credentials on their résumés and finding out who they really are. A leader listens to people, learns what they care about and what they want to do, and sees what they can become if they're given the opportunity.

There were many examples of people under my watch who benefitted from this kind of close personal attention to their career development. But I'll single out a brilliant African American woman named Julie Washington, who has worked with me in three different places. First, she headed my field marketing at Ralston Purina. She had impeccable credentials—an MBA from Washington University, an undergraduate degree from Emory University—but when she got to a middle-management position, she found herself stuck in place with no clear way to move forward, something that happens to many women of color. She was the first in her family to work in a professional job; that can mean you don't have a cousin or a sibling or a parent who can explain some of the things you should do, so you're making up your day-to-day decisions as you go along.

What I saw, however, was a professional with a passion to learn and grow, who would work sixty to seventy hours a week until the job was done. When I moved to Gillette, I recruited her to run all of our commercial marketing operations in North America, including promotional sports marketing—a job I offered her because I knew she had the potential to be great at it. And she was. Among her accomplishments, she created the celebrated Gillette Young Guns partnership with NASCAR, in which Gillette sponsored six of the racing world's top young drivers. It was an example of what happens when you talk and listen and entertain diverse ideas: Young celebrity drivers needed to be clean shaven, so why not bring them in as influencers for Gillette razors?

Later, when I went to Jamba Juice, I recruited Washington again, this time as chief marketing officer and innovation officer. She's now the chief marketing and communications officer at Trinity Health, a $27 billion health-care-delivery system, and recently landed her first board seat, at the biotech company Amyris, Inc. I'm very proud of her!

Intentional Leaders Embody These Top Ten Qualities

1. They build great teams and work environments.

2. They are mission-focused and values-based.

3. They ensure that all voices are heard.

4. They understand that leadership is a privilege and appreciate the responsibility they have in enabling each person to do their best work.

5. They understand that leaders must teach and coach; therefore they must be constant learners and good listeners.

6. They recognize and value the advantages diversity brings to solving problems and driving greater innovation.

7. They're oriented around people and teamwork; empathy and humanity are their not-so-secret superpowers.

8. They build an environment that fosters growth and development for all.

9. They appreciate and value the unique talents, backgrounds, and gifts of each team member, and strive to unlock the full potential of individuals and teams.

10. They use storytelling and company history to illustrate what's valued and what's expected in this culture, including the cultural nonnegotiables.

How I Learned to Lead

I've developed processes for creating and operationalizing an intentionally inclusive culture, which I'll discuss in detail in the chapters that follow. I began this work with the help of many bosses, many teachers, and many management gurus.

My good friend Bernard Tyson, who was the chairman and CEO of Kaiser Permanente until his untimely death, in 2019, at the age of sixty, was a shining example of what great leadership looks like. "Don't ask permission to help improve the lives of the people and communities you've pledged to serve," he said in his keynote speech at the UCLA Anderson School of Management 2019 commencement ceremony. "Instead, march through the doors of red tape, make bold moves, and usher in access for your communities to be served."[12] Those were words he lived by.

I had several notable mentors at Ralston Purina, where I worked from 1987 to 2002. One was Warner Davis, who was one of the first African Americans to become a senior executive at the company. There was another gentleman at the company, Bob Roby, and he and Warner were close friends with each other. They called themselves salt and pepper; one of them white, one African American, and at the time the mere fact that the two of them were working as sales partners was a trailblazing statement. Both were very special friends to me, supporting and encouraging me at each step—to the point that eventually, Davis ended up reporting to me for a while. He was a dear friend, and we talked almost every Sunday for over ten years. Rest in power, W. D.!

Jim Kilts, who was the chairman and CEO of Gillette when I was there, knows better than anyone how to set up a framework for a great company with an intentional culture. At Gillette he built a high-performance culture based on studying and understanding the consumer, developing great teams and talent, creating a workable playbook with a visionary strategy, and establishing a clear mission and purpose.

When I think about how I learned to be an intentional leader, however, I have to look further back, all the way to my childhood and my mother's determination to make sure I lived up to my potential.

I grew up in St. Louis with parents, James and Rose White, who instilled in me a strong work ethic. My dad worked in a printing and labeling factory. When the company moved its headquarters to Iowa, he was laid off. So he secured a job as a skycap at the St. Louis Airport. He's in his eighties now, and still working there two days a week. I asked him why he keeps working when he doesn't have to, and he said that all of it—getting up in the morning and putting on his starched shirt and polished shoes, going to the airport and looking after travelers and their baggage—gives his life focus. My mother, now retired, was a lab technician for many years. She was the one who taught me and my younger sister that you can change the trajectory of your life with education. My sister, Cheryl Jones, is now the CEO of Girls Incorporated of St. Louis.

I was the first in my family to graduate from college, but I might not have made it that far had my mother not staged an intervention when, at ten, I began to slip as a student. My grades had been good up until then, but in my fourth-grade class pandemonium reigned. The classroom was overcrowded, and the regular teacher was ill. We had four or five substitute teachers coming in throughout the year, but no one had set up a structure to follow, and the rules seemed to fly out the window. It was an early lesson to me in why culture matters, but more to the point, I was an introverted child who got completely lost in the chaos. My grades suffered, so the school administration saw me as a "slow" learner and tracked me into a semiremedial class in fifth grade.

When my mother got the news that I was going to be in a class for slow learners, a thousand alarm bells sounded. She knew it was going to be humiliating and tedious for me to be in such a class; she knew this never should have happened. Then she leaped into action. She worked with me on my studies, coached me and mentored me throughout the school year. Thanks to her I became a top student from sixth grade on. I even received an offer for a scholarship to an East Coast prep school, though ultimately, we decided I'd stay in public school. How do you take a young man at that age and put him in a slow class, and then a few years later you have academically demanding prep schools available to him? You spend a lot of time getting to understand his makeup as an individual so that you can pull the best out of him—as my mother did.

From my mother, I learned that an intentional leader teaches, cares deeply, and draws out the best in those who might otherwise be overlooked. A great leader never underestimates the human potential we all have.

An inclusive culture works both ways; the top managers are open to listening to people, and the employees are open to learning how they can bring their own unique experiences, passions, and capabilities to the job. When I was at Ralston Purina I chaired three affinity groups—internal groups of employees who shared a common identity, known in some companies as employee resource groups (ERGs). At the time we had ERGs for Black, Latinx, and female employees. In working with these groups, I learned that they could provide an excellent launch pad for people who had potential but needed more encouragement and mentoring than they were getting day-to-day. The winning formula was that we made a point of making sure every member of every group had a chance to talk about where they'd come from, what they were passionate about, and where they wanted to go in their lives and their careers. We'd have people think about their personal brands and the impressions they might be making in the work environment. We'd ask them to create action plans illustrating what they could do to contribute more to the company. I saw any number of people develop this way, softening rough edges and becoming more thoughtful about how they showed up in the world.

What I've learned in my travels is that most people are highly capable—often more capable than you might think at first sight—as long as they have a level playing field and an opportunity. Luck helps, too, but what is most important is that everyone has an environment that encourages them to reach their full potential around things that they're passionate about. And, of course, they have to be willing to put in the hard work.

I've mentioned how I encouraged Julie Washington in her career, but all I did for Julie, and others who didn't fit the conventional cultural mold, was remove the barriers so that they could come into the game. We're all used to job evaluations in the business world, in which we issue formalized pronouncements of what a person can do and what they can't do, as measured by past performance. In the kind of intentional corporate culture I'm talking about in this book, however, you make fewer pronouncements and ask more questions. When I'm evaluating employees or interviewing candidates for a job, I always want to hear their biography so that I can get a sense of the journey they've made. I want to learn how they perceive other human beings, and how inclusive they are in the world. I try to get them to describe what they're passionate about, and where they've found the most success in their careers or in school. That's how I get a sense of what will ignite them to excel to their full potential.

When it comes to potential, it was also what I had in mind when I was evaluating the organization where I became CEO—at a time when some people thought I was crazy to take a job with a company

Intentional Leadership by Design

- Be a force for positive change and the resilience it brings to your organization.
- Value all aspects of identity (diversity), ensure fair treatment and opportunity for all (equity), and bring traditionally excluded people into decision-making processes and other career-making roles (inclusion).
- Don't ask "How would this person fit in with us?" but "How would they enhance our culture?"
- Ensure that no one is overlooked or underperforming because of bias.
- Listen and ask questions instead of making pronouncements.

that was bleeding money and seemed to have a 9.5 in 10 chance of failing. "We know you want to be CEO, but why *this* company?" a number of friends said after a recruiter called asking if I'd like to interview at Jamba Juice. But when you discard preconceived notions of what works, and turn your sights to what could be there, this is where leadership for the workplace of the future begins.

2

CEO-Driven Change

My interview for the job of CEO at Jamba, Inc., couldn't have come at a more troubled time in the company's history. It was November 2008, and the Great Recession had begun to hit hard—but even before the financial crisis blew up the US economy in September of that year, Jamba had started bleeding cash. Its net losses for the previous year had been $113 million, against revenue of $400 million. The weather was turning chilly in Emeryville, California, where the company was headquartered, and that served to remind me that in most of Jamba's locations this was precisely the time of year when people would be least likely to stop at a smoothie stand for a cold, refreshing beverage.

I wasn't the board's first choice for the job, either. I arrived at 6:00 p.m., their last interview on the schedule. And after having spent much of the day interviewing a slate of candidates, they had already decided on a top choice.

I sat down with only one board member, Ramon Martin-Busutil, an operating partner from New River Capital, the firm that had led the IPO of Jamba Juice in 2006. This was apparently just a courtesy interview. But we talked for a while. I'd done my research and told him the plan I had for transforming the brand and the company. I told him that a cultural transformation was central to what I believed needed to happen—a cultural change consistent with the way I always led, seeking a staff with diverse lived experiences and a wide variety of perspectives. I told him that with more-diverse voices you can unlock more potential from the organization. After that, Martin-Busutil said he thought Steven Berrard, the chairman and interim CEO, should meet me, so he went up to Berrard's office and brought him in. That evening I ended up talking with the two of them as well as with Tom Byrne—all partners in New River Capital. They asked me to come back and meet with other board members, including Brian Swette, the former CMO of eBay and PepsiCo, and Bob Kagle, from Benchmark Capital, who had been the company's first large investor.

So in my follow-up interview, I faced a highly accomplished group of men (they were all white males), and I asked a question that, as I mentioned in chapter 1, I've heard more recently in a different context: "How could you guys have let this happen?"

I should point out that not so long before, Jamba had taken off from a simple concept to become one of the restaurant-chain industry's hottest brands. It had appeared on *Inc.* magazine's 2008 "*Inc.* 500" list of the five hundred fastest-growing private companies in the United States, based on Jamba's growth between 2004 and 2007.

Kirk Perron, an avid cyclist who liked to drink fresh-squeezed juice to replenish himself after cycling, had founded the company as a single juice stand called Juice Club, in San Luis Obispo, California, in 1990, with the idea of selling juices to bicyclists and others with an interest in healthy living. Perron expanded modestly, opening two more stores in the next couple of years. It was Bob Kagle, at Benchmark, who first saw serious growth potential. Kagle was on his way to a meeting at a restaurant one day when he spotted a Juice Club and a long line to get in. There was still a long line when he left his meeting. He contacted Perron, and it took months to convince the entrepreneur that he could build the company into something big. But Kagle finally won him over.

With capital from Benchmark and others, followed by the 2006 acquisition by Services Acquisition Corp., a special-purpose acquisition company led by Steve Berrard, the company went public and grew quickly, with more than seven hundred stores around the United States by 2007. But by mid-2007 the stock had begun to decline, and a year later it was down below $1, losing about 95 percent of its value at its height.

While the most immediate problem appeared to be a revenue decline in the midst of the economic downturn, there were also flaws in the business concept. The company was experiencing rising costs from overbuilding and was now borrowing at steep interest rates to meet its expenses. Sales were down partly because of the recession, but I also saw that the menu wasn't broad enough to sustain the restaurant chain year-round, especially with the expansion into the Midwest and the East Coast, where winters were long. Something else I observed was that there was a lack of clear direction. Board members and senior executives had plenty of big ideas, but there was no clear strategic plan. After one of my early analyst conferences, one analyst showed me the quarterly reports she'd been publishing for several years, and in each it was clear that Jamba's strategy changed almost every quarter.

At the same time, what I was thinking that day in 2008, as I looked at these distinguished directors, was that this was still a company with a purpose and tremendous potential. The brand was substantially larger than the business, which meant the company was just scratching the surface of all it was capable of doing. What it needed, in my estimation, was someone to approach it with a serious plan, not just for rapid growth but for making Jamba Juice a brand that would connect to its health-conscious customers in a deeper way, so that it would be an indispensable part of their lives. My plan included making DEI an essential part of the company's DNA. The board wanted to know how I would restore profitability and get the company on a sustainable growth trajectory that would boost the value for shareholders rather than create a culture of DEI, but my approach has always been that an intentionally inclusive organization is essential to solving problems and creating innovations in the real world.

I said that I've never been offered a job or a promotion based on my potential to rise to the occasion, but I had proven that I could build and run a much bigger consumer-products brand in the job I held at Safeway—the job I left to become CEO at Jamba. At Safeway I was running the $8 billion consumer-brands private-label portfolio, overseeing thirty factories across multiple brands and thirty-five different categories of products. I had upgraded Safeway's private-label brands into premium-price categories and expanded the organic brands, including the largest organic brand in the industry, O Organics.

I saw Jamba Juice as a company that could get back to its true north, and be far more resilient this time around, as long as those at the top developed a culture of innovation while also keeping a close watch on what was working and what wasn't. Which was why I asked that question: "How could you guys have let this happen?" I think the board decided to hire me partly because I made it clear I wouldn't have let the company slide into the state it was in.

Then I said one other thing that I think clinched the deal in my favor. "If you give me ten people," I told the board, "I'll get more out of them than nine out of ten leaders anywhere else on the planet— because I'll look to their strengths and capabilities and play to their passions."

So they hired me, and I started within a few weeks, on December 1. Now I had to live up to my words and turn the company's fortunes around. In a situation like this, you have to have a vision yet at the same time stay flexible. I started the job with a sketch of what I thought the turnaround plan should be and used the first sixty to ninety days to refine that. There was a critical plan to unlock the potential and strengths of the culture. I had a thesis about where the opportunities might be. I just didn't know what exact form the plan would take.

I did, however, know where I wanted to take the corporate culture; you can't stage a transformation without a CEO who knows what the endgame should be. And you can't separate culture from a company's financial fundamentals. Revenues, valuation, and all other numbers stem from the company's values, expectations, and mission. All operations are built around the people in the company and the way they work together and align around the mission.

So my first task was to audit the corporate culture and see what changes I'd need to make. I wanted to hear from all of the key stakeholder groups. Their feedback was critical in shaping the turnaround strategy; I knew that board members, executives, staff, franchisees, suppliers, customers, and all other key stakeholders were in a position to tell me what was needed. At the same time, I knew that having a cacophony of opinions without true leadership would only make things worse. You need big ideas—you need to bring all the ideas to the table. But ultimately, it's your job as the leader to make the final call, determining the direction you'll take and then staying true to the plan.

On my first day I began holding meetings, including a town hall with about a hundred people at the support center in Emeryville, seeking feedback from everyone. In the meetings, we passed out cards and I asked everyone to complete three sentences:

I hope James White will change: _____.

Here are two things I love about the current culture: _____

Here is one thing I'd like to preserve in the current culture: _____.

A number of people expressed a need for a greater sense of urgency, more focus on performance, and more attention to the voice of the customer when it came to product development. One almost unanimous response was that people wanted to keep the casual dress code. At Safeway, we'd all worn jackets and ties—so I adapted to a different culture, coming to work in jeans or other casual attire to match the fun and vibrant brand.

Then it was time to address culture, values, and diversity. To initiate meaningful, purposeful change, I knew I'd need the best talent out there. I'd need teams of professionals who, among them, had knowledge of the whole global range of potential consumers and how fresh-squeezed juice and smoothies and other healthy food choices could enhance their lives. I'd need people who had big ideas about innovation, but also people with expertise in spotting risks, analyzing customer preferences, and recognizing when something needed to be tweaked.

To start initiating change, I put together cross-functional action-learning teams (ALTs), striving for diversity not just in ethnic and gender balance but also across functional disciplines. This orientation is something I learned from Noel Tichy's *The Leadership Engine*. Tichy led the GE Leadership Center at its fabled corporate university, Crotonville, in the 1980s, where he oversaw GE's transformation to action learning. He has famously said that "winning organizations are teaching organizations." My interpretation of the book led me to create action-learning teams to foster continuous teaching and learning. The people on the ground are the ones who best know what's working well, and how to fix what's not, and when I brought together people who'd been on the ground in different roles, they all learned from one another about such aspects of the business as customer habits, conflicts that needed to be resolved, new food and lifestyle trends, and what competitors were doing. Powerful things happen when you bring together diverse talents to learn from one another. And when you're a leader, one of your most important roles is to develop other leaders who can make decisions and initiate the required changes in their area.

ALTs can make a big difference when it comes to innovation and problem-solving, but to actually make them a part of the cultural transformation, I purposely chose previously overlooked employees to be part of the teams. As a result, the teams were far more diverse than the company's workforce as a whole. My colleague Joan Williams, a professor and the founding director of the Center for WorkLife Law at the University of California's Hastings College of the Law, called the ALTs "glamour work" in an article we coauthored for *Harvard Business Review*.[1] These are glamour assignments in the sense that they're line roles that get attention, generate revenue, and prepare people for greater responsibilities within the company—and these are just the kind of assignments that in conventional corporate environments would most often go to young white males based on management's view of their potential.

Typically, middle-level managers are the ones who decide who gets these high-profile assignments, and if most of the middle-level managers are white men, they will often pick the junior staffers they most relate to. It's the informal systems of who gets invited to certain meetings, who gets invited to work on critical projects. Even if there is a chief diversity officer to encourage diversity hires, that person has little control over who gets these coveted assignments—unless the CDO is also the CEO or is working closely with the CEO in an organization in which C-level executives handpick people who can eventually become part of a diverse pipeline to senior management positions.

The underpinning of all of this is a CEO who sets the tone and requires that all senior managers and middle managers make DEI one of their business priorities—not just because it's the right thing to do, but because more-diverse teams are going to transform the way the company solves problems and expands.

I think we're far more aware of the need to overcome unconscious biases now than most corporate leaders were in 2008—but we're just starting to see how wide a net you cast when you have a culture of DEI. When I became the CEO of Jamba Juice, I inherited a company that was founded by a gay man and was generally welcoming to the LGBTQIA+ community. However, it isn't hard to find workplaces that have plenty of white women, as well as gay men and women, in leadership roles, but few people of color of any gender. Nor have many companies gone out of their way to open up to transgender and gender-nonconforming people.

Furthermore, representation without true inclusion is incomplete. What I'm saying is, DEI is a continuous experience in checking your unconscious biases, learning from people you might otherwise overlook, and intentionally bringing in people with a variety of cultural perspectives. When you take this approach, you get a wider, better range of ideas. True, it usually takes a while for the team to come together, but when it does, you get better problem-solving. The focus on culture is all about the team rather than individuals. There's rarely one big, magic moment when someone says "Eureka!" and the skies part. What did happen at Jamba Juice, though, was that our diverse teams had big ideas for turning the company into a healthy-lifestyle brand that reached into new communities and venues.

When I became CEO, most Jamba shops were in strip and shopping malls and urban commercial centers—places that might be destinations for loyal customers. Our diverse ALTs came up with the idea that we should reach out to more consumers on their own turf. So we opened Jamba Juice stores on more college campuses, and we went into K–12 schools, including many in underserved neighborhoods, honing a role for the company as a solution provider in schools looking for healthier food and beverage options. We added steel-cut oatmeal and sandwiches to the menu, so that Jamba could be a breakfast and lunch destination. We added hot beverages to appeal to customers in colder climates at any time of year. We brought Jamba Juice concessions to school, community, and sporting events, a way of reinforcing our commitment to communities. The ALTs determined that there was a market for juice smoothies and healthy snacks in Asia, and among travelers in general, so we expanded globally and more than tripled our presence in airports.

Founder Kirk Perron himself joined our continuous-learning effort as a resource when Starbucks announced it was going to start serving juices and we needed to develop a strategy to meet this competition head-on. We were able to compete successfully because of brand strength; people associated Jamba Juice with overall healthy lifestyles. We had celebrity athletes like Venus Williams and Vernon Davis as franchise partners and spokespeople, and it helped that our founder was closely associated with an active lifestyle.

Sadly, Perron died in June 2020, an untimely death at the age of fifty-six, apparently of cardiac arrest. He was a true visionary. I can only say that he lived well and created a brand that just might be strong enough to outlive us all. (Now known as just Jamba, it was acquired by Focus Brands in 2018.)

Just as notable as the redesign of Jamba Juice's business strategy was the purposeful culture that we created. Our action-learning-team members brought insights on social and environmental initiatives that they cared about, and we developed a few programs that helped make Jamba Juice more of a company that mattered in the lives of people. To name a few of the things we did, we were partners in the Obama administration's "Let's Move!" campaign, dedicated to solving the problem of childhood obesity by creating a healthier start for children, and we launched our own "Team Up for a Healthy America" initiative to encourage adults and children to adopt healthier diets, with Venus Williams—who owned several Jamba Juice stores herself—as a celebrity spokesperson. Through the Department of Labor's Job Corps program, we sponsored vocational training at the Treasure Island Advanced Culinary Arts program in San Francisco.

With many of our stores on board to participate in reducing carbon emissions, we started a project to lower our electricity usage, and we introduced food containers, utensils, and napkins all made from recyclable materials.

These projects served an additional purpose: they made Jamba an exciting, cool place to work, and helped create bonds within a diverse pool of employees. In the traditional corporate world, you have executives who know one another well, through family connections and old school ties, from playing golf together and belonging to the same clubs and churches. Needless to say, in a diverse leadership team, people don't get hired or promoted through these types of social connections. Socializing with colleagues outside of work has never been a big component of how I work, but I've found more-constructive ways to have people come together in community. At Jamba we brought our associates together for company outreach work—for example, coastal cleanups, planting gardens at schools, and spending time with young people through Junior Achievement. We sponsored half-marathons—I ran in several, even though I hadn't run in a marathon before—and that was a chance for our staff to mingle and feel that they had personal stakes in our healthy-lifestyle brand.

Now, when you take the helm at a troubled company and announce that you're going to be making big changes, inevitably there are going to be people who don't want to see things change. I've always addressed those who resist with a combination of patience and a few requirements that are nonnegotiable. On the one hand, transformation is a multiyear journey, and some detractors will come around when they begin to see how well it works. On the other hand, I let everyone know from the start that we are going to treat all people in the organization with respect, we are going to unbias our systems (more on that in the chapters that follow), we are going to educate ourselves about unconscious biases, and we are going to be more inclusive in our hiring and assignments. If you find these conditions problematic, you probably need to go, but otherwise give transformation a try.

In resetting the culture at Jamba Juice, I set high expectations for performance—i.e., results—and I demanded inclusive cross-functional teamwork, with leaders who were aligned with this way of working. I knew when I came in that not everyone was going to be a fit with the new corporate culture. I changed about a third of the leadership team within the first six months. For the most part, we mutually agreed that it was time for them to go. In asking for manager engagement, I particularly targeted middle-level managers. At every organization I've helped lead, I've found that middle-level managers really hold the key to delivering cultural change, because they control the work experience of everyone in the chain of command below them. I designed a new incentive system, in which up to 20 percent of store managers' compensation was determined by engagement, climate, and organizational health scores, using a variant of the Gallup Q^{12} survey to measure employee engagement and performance outcomes.

At the same time, however, if you are leading this kind of transformation, it's equally critical to have diversity at the top; that way you not only show all stakeholders what a true meritocracy looks like but you also populate the board and management with people who are likely to support the structural changes you want to accomplish. In my first year at Jamba Juice we brought two women onto the board, one of whom was African American. When I started at the company, management was 80 percent white men; by the end of my first year, half of the managers were women and people of color. Within three years the company's market cap had soared by 500 percent.

A diverse culture performs better because the more variety you have in thinking and expertise, and the greater the variety of people you have in a room, the more innovation you'll have, along with better awareness of trends, markets, and risk. I am confident that the new range of voices on our board changed the way the company thought about its people and its business. With a less diverse board, my overall plan for structural changes might not have been supported in the same way.

Why the CEO Must Be in Charge of DEI

I've related my story because I've heard from so many business leaders who want to know how I created a culture of DEI and how they can do it.

The first step, always, is to have a CEO who is wholly invested in building a corporate culture in which people are the most valued assets—in everyday practice, not just in a marketing campaign—and everyone in management understands that it's their job to develop all of their employees as leaders, innovators, and problem-solvers. Companies waste millions of dollars developing diversity and antibias training programs to throw at the problem. Training isn't going to stick unless the CEO and senior leadership team practice DEI every minute of every day and make it clear that this is how we work: with inclusive leaders who teach, unlock talent, and focus on building a great environment for all.

I have always tried to model this kind of intentional, inclusive management style in everything I do and say. I demonstrate it to my management teams through details, such as who gets to be sitting in the room when we make important decisions and who is assigned to the most-prestigious projects. Also very important is that the CEO encourages everyone in the room to speak and listens to what they're saying. All too often, in all too many companies, we hear of women and minorities presenting an important idea in a meeting, but no one actually recognizes the idea until a white male repeats it. When I witness that happening, I say, "John, I'm glad you support the idea that Sally presented."

It is becoming an increasingly common practice to hire a chief diversity officer (CDO)—often someone who is a woman and/or a person of color themselves—as a way of showing that the company is committed to achieving DEI. But where many companies have stopped short is that the CDO doesn't have enough authority to change a culture where bias is a way of life. Typically, the company creates the role as a reaction to problems with race-related issues or sexual misconduct. From there, the CDO is set up to be unsuccessful in bringing on real change.

Here's why: CDOs tend to have relatively short tenures, in most places not more than a year or two, and little in the way of meaningful resources or influence. In most organizations, CDOs don't own any of the relevant HR systems, much less all of them. You might eliminate bias in one system, but it remains in place everywhere else. Indeed, the person in the CDO role might be there mostly as window dressing in a company that has suffered from discrimination scandals, and sometimes they become little more than the scapegoat for initiatives that fail to measure up.

That's why I say the cultural transformation has to come from the top. It is possible to have an effective CDO, but that person has to be a part of the senior leadership team and have the resources and authority to address all aspects of company policy, operations, and strategy, and to change both formal and informal systems. Along with the CDO's authority, it falls to everyone in senior management to demonstrate on a daily basis what an inclusive corporate culture looks like.

You might say I appointed myself as chief diversity officer at Jamba Juice, very deliberately seeking out both official assignments and off-site projects that would help bring out the best capabilities among diverse talents who'd been overlooked because they didn't fit the conventional mold. My goal was to make DEI so deeply ingrained that we didn't need a CDO to carry out policies. That works at a company the size of Jamba Juice. At larger companies, the CEO should still drive the effort, but would probably need to delegate some aspect of the day-to-day work.

Anti-Racist Leadership

At Nielsen, the global marketing-research and audience-rating firm, CEO David Kenny has also given himself the official title of chief diversity officer. Nielsen has a senior executive in charge of diversity and inclusion, but as Kenny told CNBC in June 2020, he took on the role himself to make sure that the discussion of diversity and equality "is front and center in the board room and in the management room," with the ability to measure outcomes in a similar way to measuring financial results.[2]

The role seems to come naturally to him. Kenny is an outspoken champion for diversity and social justice; even outside of work he has been an activist on behalf of immigrants to the United States. He filed an amicus brief with the Supreme Court opposing the citizenship question on the 2020 census, which would have potentially discouraged minority participation. Kenny brought together industry bodies to petition the court—which ultimately did order that the citizenship question be removed.

He has said that as the largest global ratings organization, Nielsen needs to be sure it weighs the perspectives of *all* of its consumers and partners, and all of its 44,000 employees across one hundred countries. The company has scored 100 percent on the Human Rights Campaign (HRC) Foundation's Corporate Equality Index for many years, and in 2019 it scored 100 percent on the Disability Equality Index. In response to the spring 2020 uprisings for racial justice, Kenny urged leaders to take this as an opportunity to embed DEI into their organizations. He also underscored the importance of humility for a leader striving to be truly anti-racist and said that people in power must acknowledge the existence of systemic racism.

Among the accountability measures he's taken, Kenny has tied executive incentives to DEI contributions and has set the expectation that everyone who manages people must be active in the employee-resource-group programs and must make personal contributions to diversity and inclusion a part of performance reviews. He has also started a pro bono consulting program for minority-owned businesses.

"Particularly if you are a CEO or in the C-suite, a lot of power and responsibility comes with the job—so you have to be sure to address the system and not just individuals," Kenny told Yahoo Finance. "Then you need to develop an action plan to address racism both for individuals inside your company and the systemic racism in society. We are on our way at Nielsen, but this will be a long road and I'm committed to working at this as long as it takes."[3] The CEO is the only party with the authority to overhaul systemic racism and other biases this way—and elevate the importance of the DEI agenda to the point that it becomes a critical business initiative, linked to reward systems and expectation setting for everyone in the organization.

Other CEOs Who've Shaken the Corporate World

Corporate culture reveals itself in a crisis, and when the multiple crises of 2020 hit, it became very clear who was exhibiting the kind of leadership that's needed for these times. While there are many praiseworthy CEOs—and many whose work I'll discuss in this book—there are three who spring most immediately to mind when I think of those who have a playbook for building the kind of intentionally inclusive culture that makes an organization resilient and who have been leading with a clear voice in this moment.

Brian Cornell, chairman and CEO of Target

I've mentioned that Brian Cornell is leading a highly intentional transformation. His efforts began when he took over as CEO of Target in 2014, and he's always been a leader who tests his policies from the ground up. He walks around stores unannounced so that he can observe the shopping experience and the way salesclerks are interacting with customers and one another. In steering his company through the challenges of systemic racism, he hasn't missed a beat. The best management teams can shift seamlessly from one crisis to the next when they have to.

Actually, Target was holding listening sessions for employees to talk about race issues for four years before the George Floyd killing. After that crisis, however, some seven thousand employees gathered virtually for a series of open dialogues. One of the stories they heard about racism came from Kamau Witherspoon, a senior vice president of operations at Target. As reported by *The Wall Street Journal*, one ordinary evening in 2008, Witherspoon went jogging and then went home and was loading his dishwasher when he noticed flashlights pointed at his window. There, in his backyard, were four police officers, and when he reached to open the window to talk to them, three pointed guns at him. Apparently, the police were responding to a call from a neighbor saying a Black man was running through the neighborhood—and that alone aroused suspicion. "I'm sharing this story with you to get you to understand how significant of an issue it is, how much of a burden that I carry, the Black leaders and team members carry in our stores . . . We're exhausted, and this is why we're exhausted," Witherspoon told a group of Target executives.[4]

Their boss, meanwhile, was showing his support with money and actions. Under Cornell's leadership, the company also made a $10 million commitment to donate to organizations working for Black communities. Cornell also put out a statement in support of the Minneapolis protesters who fought for justice after the murder of George Floyd, despite the property damage done to some Target stores. "We are a community in pain," he said before announcing that Target teams were preparing truckloads of first-aid equipment and medicine, bottled water, baby formula, diapers, and other essentials to help ensure that no one within the areas of heaviest damage and demonstration was cut off from needed supplies.[5]

When he isn't addressing a national crisis, Cornell is leading the company through a wide range of aggressive climate and energy goals in its 1,800 stores and its global supply chain. Employees are encouraged to develop ideas and skills for the future of the planet, with ongoing training that has given teams the autonomy to design and promote new products.

Bernard Tyson, former chairman and CEO of Kaiser Permanente

Bernard Tyson was one of the first CEOs to put the issue of race front and center; at the time something of a lone voice. In fact, he pretty much defined the difference between diversity and inclusion in a talk with *Fortune* editor, Clifton Leaf, at the 2019 Great Place to Work for All Summit, an annual event held by the workplace-culture consulting firm Great Place to Work. (Tyson died later the same year, at the age of sixty.) He pointed out that for many companies, diversity is essentially a number count. You might have an acceptable number of high-ranking women and people of color, "but the dominant culture has already decided what the environment is going to feel like, operate, and you have to assimilate, and you have to become one . . . So we work very hard on the inclusiveness, which is, you have a right to be at the table, you have a right to be who you are, you have a right to think the way you think, and the objective here is to celebrate diversity and get all the different perspectives and walks of life and different ways of looking at issues and challenges, because we're all working towards the same end point, which is the mission of the organization."[6]

Tyson was out there blogging that it was "time to revolutionize race relations" after the grand jury declined to indict police officer Darren Wilson for the shooting of Michael Brown in 2014, and again issued calls for unity after yet another round of police shootings of unarmed Black men. When President Trump issued an executive order banning immigrants from seven largely Muslim countries, Tyson sent a message to his employees promising that Kaiser would not discriminate.

Jason Wingard, writing in *Forbes*, praised how Tyson led the health-care industry in creating "a total health agenda that prioritized preventative medicine and accounted for lifestyle variations" instead of simply focusing on hospitals or treatments. That translated to such innovations as farmers markets in urban areas where healthy food was hard to come by, a $200 million fund to address homelessness by creating affordable housing, and a medical school where doctors were taught "how to take care of the whole person and how the person fits into the environment."[7]

Tyson was vocal about his own experiences with bias, letting the business world know that the best way to fight it was to bring it out into the open. In an episode of the Spotify podcast *Pivot to the Future*, recorded shortly before his death, Tyson talked frankly about a certain unnamed medical director who was his partner when he was a hospital administrator at Kaiser—and how from day one, the two of them just didn't get along. One day they agreed to have a heart-to-heart talk about why. It turned out, said Tyson, that the medical director had "never had to work closely with a Black professional . . . he didn't have a mental road map of how to deal with me. That has been a lesson for me, that it might not be racist, it might be struggling. There are opportunities to help bring people along, and to create new road maps to how to look at me as an individual." The good news, he added, was that afterward, he and the medical director had "the most terrific relationship."[8]

I saw how Tyson put that same lesson out to the world. We could really use him in this moment, but a leader who creates a strong corporate culture can expect his or her legacy to live on in the DNA of the organization, and I've been pleased to see that happen under Greg Adams, the chairman and CEO who succeeded Tyson, and other senior leaders. Kaiser has consistently scored as one of the top workplaces for diversity and inclusion and ranks as one of the Human Rights Campaign's best places to work for LGBTQIA+ equality.

Lisa Wardell, former chairman and CEO, now executive chair, of Adtalem Global Education

One of the few Black women CEOs in the entire S&P 400 index of mid-cap companies, Lisa Wardell headed up one of the country's largest for-profit college chains, with a focus on training medical, health-care, and financial professionals. I'm a director and former chairman of the board at Adtalem, and I watched Wardell reposition the organization as a strategic workforce-solutions enterprise, improve the cost base and the balance sheet, and assemble a world-class leadership team. I think of her as a CEO who was built for this moment of multiple crises.

She became CEO at a time when the company, then known as DeVry Education Group, was facing reputational damage due to a lawsuit and was in serious need of a turnaround. We knew she had what it took to change the culture and steer the company to the future. She has said she took the job mostly because Robert Johnson, the founder of Black Entertainment Television who was a trusted mentor to her, advised her that this was an opportunity that so few Black people get. She more than rose to the occasion. She settled the suit and gave the company a fresh start, repositioning our brand and our portfolio of businesses, with a corporate culture that under her leadership became more decisive and urgent, and more focused on financial performance. She led the higher-education sector in implementing new standards in transparency and financial literacy, and she tried to produce medical professionals who were willing to work in underserved communities. Under her leadership, gender and ethnic diversity increased at the Adtalem board to 62 percent and within Adtalem's senior leadership to 78 percent. On the board, four of the ten directors are African American, and three of the five committees are chaired by African Americans, including me.

Wardell also made Adtalem a company that aims to fill critical global-workforce needs. The subsidiary Chamberlain University, particularly known for its school of nursing, graduates one out of every thirty-four nurses in the United States, and a disproportionate number of Black and Latinx nurses. She instituted a much more thoughtful way of building a pipeline of diverse students into the medical and financial professions—for example, through relationships she formed with historically Black colleges and universities.

In 2017, Wardell faced another test of her leadership: two category 5 hurricanes battered two of her Caribbean campuses in just two weeks. She quickly organized a way to keep her damaged medical school going—on a cruise ship in the harbor, where more than one thousand students were able to live and take classes for two months. Who else would think of that?

She was no less quick to come up with a crisis-response strategy when the Covid-19 pandemic and the George Floyd tragedy struck. Adtalem, through its Global Education Foundation, gave a total of $300,000 in donations to a health-care organization and a financial-services organization aimed at fighting poverty in Chicago, where Adtalem is headquartered. Many corporations have foundations and philanthropic programs, but Wardell was particularly savvy about aligning hers with the school's mission.

The statement she sent out after the George Floyd killing was highly personal. "As the proud mother of black teenage sons, I am gripped with fear for their safety, deeply anxious that the sheer ran-domness of this bigoted violence might ensnare them and threaten their lives," she wrote. "And as the chairman & CEO of Adtalem Global Education—a family of organizations that prides itself on its diver-sity & inclusion and its culture of access, empowerment, and care—I am more resolute than ever in the need for our community of col-leagues, students, members and customers to do our part to ensure that our values are reflected in the communities where we learn, work and live."[9]

If there weren't CEOs who felt they had a personal stake in foster-ing a better climate for race relations—whether it's because they've encountered bias firsthand or they just understand that it's good business to be on the right side of an inclusive society—no one else in the executive suites would feel entirely safe sticking their necks out to support the Black Lives Matter movement. And even in less tumul-tuous times, while forward-thinking managers in some divisions might recruit and train more-diverse pools of talent, no one other than the CEO would have the authority to say we are going to embrace diversity by changing our board composition and the way we iden-tify people to fill our most critical assignments.

All of this became much clearer when the country spun into a twofold crisis. Business leaders began to see that a corporate culture that closes off diverse ideas and talents leaves even good people ill-equipped to know what to do, because they don't have lived experiences that allow them to lead their workforce and respond to consumer needs in ways that answer the problems we're facing. But during this crisis crunch, I met with any number of CEOs who recognized that they were going to have to change their culture in order to thrive, and who are now on their way to becoming some of the notable leaders of the future.

One CEO to watch is Leslie Stretch, of Medallia, a $6 billion market-cap company that makes customer-experience software, based in San Francisco. As a response to the Black Lives Matter demonstrations in 2020, Stretch contacted me because he recognized that the composition of the company needed to look more like the population as a whole, and I've since joined the board. As of June 2020, only 1 percent of Medallia's US employees self-identified as Black or African American, and Stretch wants to gradually increase that presence to 13 percent by 2023—corresponding with the representation in the United States as a whole. He invited me to provide some unfiltered advice at a digital town hall for his more than one thousand employees around the world.

It was a very productive meeting. Stretch started out by saying that "the status quo is not that good."

I talked about some of my lived experiences as an African American executive. For example, in my first job out of college I was a sales rep for the Minute Maid division of Coca-Cola in Springfield, Missouri, and the managers changed my territory because it had previously covered the town of Harrison, Arkansas, which was suspected of being the national headquarters for the Ku Klux Klan. On several occasions, when I called on supermarkets in some small towns, the retail managers would tell me, "We heard you were in town, and we suggest you not go out after dark." These were all-white communities that used to be known as "sundown towns," with official decrees that any

Black visitors must be out by sundown. As I learned, these places continued to exist well after the passage of the Civil Rights Act and the abolishment (at least in theory) of Jim Crow laws. And I talked about a time that I was promoted to a vice president position, but only after I was in charge of 70 percent of the division's business—in essence, I was already performing the job of a vice president rather than being promoted on my potential. I told the audience that if we're going to promote people based on their potential, let's make sure everyone has the opportunity to be evaluated based on their potential to achieve.

I told the Medallians, as the employees and executives call themselves, much the same things that I've told leaders in other industries. Consider where you're recruiting talent. About 25 percent of all STEM graduates come out of historically Black colleges and universities, so those are places where a tech CEO should have a recruiting strategy. I suggested taking key projects and surgically placing diverse talent in those projects in order to accelerate the careers of those people. They'll have broader exposure to the highest-priority company projects, and they'll be able to demonstrate their leadership, all of which will create its own upward momentum.

This is how you begin to develop a corporate culture in which DEI is so omnipresent that people identify first and foremost, at least when they're at work, as members of this dynamic organization, connected to one another through their passion for creating the best possible products and services for a brand they're proud to be part of. That's why inclusive companies tend to perform better over the long term. In the chapters that follow, I'll lay out the game plan for getting there.

Key Takeaway

A DEI transformation must be intentional and must be led by the CEO.

Checklist for CEOs

✓ Design a culture of inclusiveness with the aim of better problem-solving and better innovations.

✓ Create cross-functional action-learning teams (ALTs), striving for diversity not just in ethnic and gender balance but also across functional disciplines.

✓ Make DEI a continuous experience, checking your unconscious biases, learning from people you might otherwise overlook, and intentionally bringing in people with a variety of cultural perspectives.

✓ Recognize that without a CEO who has a personal stake in fostering a better climate for race relations and an inclusive society, no one else will feel safe sticking their necks out.

✓ If your status quo isn't diverse and inclusive, acknowledge that you will seek to do better.

3

How to Begin

Transforming to an intentionally inclusive culture is going to require several years of effort. "Where do we even start?" more than one CEO has asked me.

My answer is always this: Before you throw money at the diversity problem, before you embark on a new program of big strategic changes or do anything else, the company's senior leaders, especially including the CEO, need to look inward. Ask yourselves: *Can I put myself in the shoes of others who might be coming to their jobs every day from a different lived experience?*

Imagining someone else's perspective isn't always as easy as it might sound. Yet it all begins with one not-always-simple action: It must start with empathy at the top—or the effort will fail.

When I brought up this critical element to Krista, she stopped me in midsentence. "It's easy to talk about empathy," she said. "But we all know that it doesn't come naturally to some people. How does a business leader develop empathy if it isn't already there?"

I realized that many chief executives are going to need to build their capabilities when it comes to empathy. When you've spent years, maybe your whole life, in a position of privilege, you don't always realize that this *is* privilege and that your view from the front office is different from that of others. But you can think of empathy as a skill that anyone can master through the S-curve framework that is used in many disciplines to represent the beginning, rapid growth, and maturity of learning. It requires stepping outside of your comfort zone and embracing change. But I do believe it's a business skill that every leader has to recognize and continually polish. I've seen it happen.

My approach to empathy "training" has sometimes meant just dropping executives into a total-immersion experience. For example, when I was at Nestlé Purina, and later when I was at Gillette, on several occasions I asked white associates to accompany me to conferences hosted by such organizations as the National Society of Hispanic MBAs (NSHMBA) and the National Black MBA Association. Inevitably, my white colleague would confide to me afterward, "It was so uncomfortable being the only white person in the room."

"That's what it's like for some of us every single day," I'd reply.

I should point out that the main purpose of going to these conferences wasn't to make a few white executives learn how it feels to be underrepresented, but—instead—to dispel the notion that it's hard to find diverse talent. I'd explain to my colleagues that I'm going to take you to a place that has thousands of talented Latinx and Black folks with MBAs from some of the most prestigious universities and colleges on the planet. It was also an educational process for white colleagues to spend a couple of days walking in someone else's shoes, hearing about the business world from people who didn't look quite like them. But the part about learning how it felt to be in the minority was a powerful lesson too. I also took male associates to women's conferences, and the reaction was generally similar. One executive who worked for me at Nestlé Purina was so stressed out after spending a full day as one of a handful of men at a conference of about five hundred women, he said he just couldn't bring himself to go out to dinner with the group that night.

I'm going to borrow some additional suggestions about cultivating empathy from Lisa Wardell, the former CEO of Adtalem Global Education. I've already mentioned that she was a CEO who was made for this moment. She's told me that she's always intentional about the way she expresses empathy, and she's also a great model for how to develop this skill. "I know people are watching the CEO for cues," she says. "Are you asking the person in the mailroom and the janitor how their families are doing, just as you do when you walk past a vice president's office?"[1]

She has made it clear, by her message about her own sons (see chapter 2), that anti-racism is a personal matter to her. But she followed up that statement with a message for all of those who might not have gone through life braced at every minute for discrimination and violence, with advice about how to strengthen their empathy and how to engage with colleagues in conversations about sensitive topics like racial inequity and social justice. She urged her audience to recognize that others have different life experiences and to approach the conversation "eager to learn, not as an expert." She offered concrete actions they could take to support diversity at large—join, volunteer at, or donate to an organization that fights for social justice; support Black-owned businesses; make it known within your networks that you are seeking to mentor diverse talent and be open to accepting a mentoring request from a person of color.

Empathy comes from hearing other people's stories, so it isn't surprising that Wardell and other business leaders at the forefront of cultural change have also recommended books, articles, and movies to their managers and employees. (See my list in the appendix.) But there's another reason to present your staff with a reading list: if you've all read the same book or books on the subject of race, you can start talking with a common language and a common set of beliefs as a guide to where you need to go.

Getting others on board with a shared message is the first step in building empathy throughout the organization. The best way to ensure empathy, and make it sustainable, is to put in place an organizational infrastructure that facilitates the expression of empathy. You can incorporate it into your internal processes, so that the company's senior leaders show others in the company that this is the way we do business.

Philip Marineau, who was the CEO at Levi's from 1999 to 2006, made empathy part of the company's core value statement: "Empathy, integrity, originality, and courage." Larry Ruff worked at Levi's for twenty-five years, ultimately as chief strategy and business-development officer, and was a force behind bringing in domestic-partner benefits for LGBTQIA+ employees. "We brought empathy into employee reviews, where your empathy skills were part of the performance being assessed," says Ruff, who is now the president and chief operating officer at fair-trade-products certifier Fair Trade USA. "That forced people to see the perspective of others—not just internally, but also the perspective of customers and other stakeholders."[2]

Most of all, though, you build your empathy skills by listening. When I advise business leaders on DEI, I tell them to understand the importance of empathy and then start listening to others. Listen more than you talk, know that you don't have all of the answers, and be humble enough to let your employees and stakeholders know that this is a journey for everyone, including those at the top. That is what I saw Medallia CEO Leslie Stretch doing in a highly effective way. Medallia's B2B software is designed to help client companies understand their customers better, so empathy is a crucial component of their technology, and Stretch has told me he believes it's important to expand the concept to the workplace.

When I addressed the Medallia managers and told them that I had never, in my entire career, been promoted based on my potential, I could see the quizzical faces on the Zoom screen. This is something that never occurs to most white people. The idea that you're promoted into a role because you've shown potential to do more, to be more, is something that's just assumed by many who've lived that reality. It simply doesn't compute that there are people who are not promoted this way—it was as if I had said two plus two equals five. This is why empathy is so critical. Opening yourself to these experiences, listening to those who've lived different realities from yours, is the only way to build the baseline understanding of what's going on and what needs to be done.

It's important to recognize, too, that the path to empathy is operational and deliberate. You don't get there just by announcing that there's going to be a policy of talking things out; you create a structure for learning how others feel. Structure comes through policies and programs, and normalizing behaviors that create empathy.

Anti-Racist Leadership

Treat empathy-building as you would any product or system launch, testing your strategy in one place, working out the details, and creating a structure for how you'll unleash it. We've all seen cautionary tales from launches that happen prematurely, and you might remember such a tale from Starbucks. I am a big fan of the work that Howard Schultz tried to do in this area when he was CEO of the café chain. I admire the heart and soul he put into his leadership. Unfortunately, what the world remembers best is the heartfelt but ham-handed attempt he made to foster more understanding through the short-lived Race Together campaign of March 2015.

It began as a response to the killings of two unarmed black men the summer before: Michael Brown, in Ferguson, Missouri, and Eric Garner, on Staten Island, New York. The idea was that baristas at Starbucks coffee shops across the United States would write "Race Together" on the beverage cups, inviting customers to have a conversation about race. It was a starting point; Schultz was ahead of his time in his efforts to speak out about racial inequality at various forums, maintaining that corporations have obligations to society beyond just making profits. He spoke out on this years before the Business Roundtable released its famous 2019 statement to the same effect. The Race Together campaign, however, ran into such a barrage of skepticism and social-media vitriol that Schultz scaled down the campaign just a week after starting it, and then let it fizzle out.

The flaws in the campaign had partly to do with logistics; no one tested it to see how it would work in practice. As it turned out, customers said it was asking a lot to have a serious conversation about such a sensitive subject before they'd even downed their morning java jolt, while baristas found it difficult just to stop and write out *Race*

Together in the middle of a busy shift, let alone allow the line of customers to grow longer while they stopped to talk about the meaning and implications of racism. But the strategic glitch was that, in spite of all good intentions, the campaign lacked both structure and leadership. You can't just free-float the idea of doing something about racism into an organization without first creating a framework for the discussion. It is also important to have an end goal; that is, quantify your findings, and create a process for solving the problem.

I'm happy to see that Starbucks is now doing all of that. In this new era, under CEO Kevin Johnson, the coffee chain has announced it will aim to have people of color fill at least 30 percent of its US corporate staff and 40 percent of its US retail and manufacturing staff by 2025. Rosalind Brewer, who was the company's chief operating officer from 2017 to 2021, is a dynamo who did a great job of troubleshooting during another notorious mishap, helping set Starbucks on a course to being a company at the forefront of anti-racism. Now the CEO of Walgreens Boots Alliance, Brewer is an African American woman who pops up on almost every list of the most powerful women in business. After Starbucks came under fire in 2018 for the arrest of two Black men who were sitting in a Philadelphia store—waiting for a business meeting, as it turned out—Johnson issued an apology, and Brewer got in front of the media. "We're looking at ourselves first and saying, how can we be better, and how can we do better?" she said in a National Public Radio interview.[3] Starbucks followed up with policy changes that included mandatory antibias training for executives and tying compensation to diversity metrics. It took courage to institute these policies at the time, because Starbucks is a federal contractor and made the announcement in spite of both an executive order from the Trump

White House barring federal grant recipients from conducting diversity training and a threat that the administration might cancel contracts with companies that violated the order.

In the spring of 2020, Kevin Johnson brought some two thousand Starbucks partners together for a virtual discussion about racial injustice and the murders of George Floyd, Ahmaud Arbery, and Breonna Taylor. A CEO letter that remains on the company's website makes the case for empathy, and for listening as a cornerstone of diversity, with inspiration from Dr. Martin Luther King Jr.'s quotation: "A riot is the language of the unheard. And what is it that America has failed to hear?"

As business leaders we might also ask: "What is it that corporate America has failed to hear? What is it that my own company has failed to hear?" These are questions to keep in mind as you embark on the process of transforming your corporate culture. I've developed a playbook for this, adopted from my own experience and from discussions with other business leaders who have nailed this transformation. It begins with seven steps that I discuss in depth below:

1. Actively listen and learn

2. Enlist and align across the senior leadership team

3. Audit the culture

4. Document what you're doing now

5. Establish benchmarks

6. Build action-learning teams or task forces

7. Develop an action plan

Actively Listen and Learn

By actively listening and learning, I mean set up a formal process for taking the pulse of the organization. I've worked with CEOs who have set up town halls at which anywhere from one hundred to one thousand or more employees can start talking and listening. Those CEOs have also organized more-intimate roundtable discussions with smaller groups, typically of fifteen to twenty. You too can use both formats. Either way, think of this as a listening tour that gives the CEO a chance to hear from people at all levels of the organization.

The way a town hall is structured will depend on whether your staffers are mostly in the same geographic area, in which case you can bring everyone into an assembly hall with speakers on stage, or whether they're spread out and can only assemble virtually. Typically, the meeting will last between forty-five and ninety minutes. You might start with a discussion of company values, led by the CEO or another senior leader in the organization. It can also be highly effective to have a guest speaker or a small panel of speakers discussing topics related to diversity and inclusion. After the discussion, you invite the audience—the employees, that is—to ask questions.

At roundtable meetings, the idea is for the CEO to listen to what the attendees have to say. The meetings can be in person or virtual and should include associates at every level, with participants from a variety of divisions and job functions. If you have factories or warehouses, plan to visit them and invite both managers and workers to the discussions. If your operations are far-flung, a series of face-to-face meetings of small groups will require the CEO to embark on a heavy travel schedule for two or three months—an investment of time that I guarantee will produce quantifiable returns over the long term through new innovations and new ways of solving problems.

In both formats, your key objectives are twofold. The first goal is that the CEO and other senior leaders engage with staff members, perhaps at levels the leaders haven't tried before, to hear what's going on in the hearts and minds of their employee base. Be prepared to use these sessions to give voice to those who have been voiceless within the organization. The only way to find out who has been voiceless is to be open to listening—and to conceding that all is not right. In her highly acclaimed book *Caste: The Origins of Our Discontents*, journalist Isabel Wilkerson points out that in order to transform, you have to identify old ills, similar to the way a doctor needs to know a patient's medical history in order to treat the symptoms. (See "More Resources for Understanding Racism" in the appendix.)

I know what many business leaders think at this stage. How are employees going to feel safe speaking so freely to the CEO? The answer is that of course, you can't always expect breakthrough discussions in your first listen-and-learn sessions. No doubt it will be difficult to get meaningful, constructive feedback in a room filled with people from multiple levels. In most workplaces people are used to a hierarchy and to limits on how much they can safely speak their minds. Still, I like to have these open forums at which everyone is encouraged to speak up, because it's a way of showing that I'm trying to create a shift in the culture. I'm working with a number of CEOs now who started with companywide meetings and then set up other venues that employees can use to follow up—anonymously if they prefer. Venues for continued feedback might come in the form of surveys, internal blogs, Slack channels, or messages that are filtered through a point person in HR, who then distills the findings and passes them along to senior management.

Lisa Wardell started conducting listen-and-learn meetings before the George Floyd murder and subsequent shakeup, and she received honest feedback in the form of follow-up messages and emails. After a series of companywide discussions about Black Lives Matter and police brutality, she received a message from an employee who wrote, "My spouse is a police officer, and I don't appreciate your talking about police brutality this way."

"I think that's the brave person," said Wardell, who made sure that the company had platforms that allow everyone to express opinions of all kinds.[4]

When I started at Jamba Juice and held town halls and roundtable meetings to get a sense of where we stood, culturally speaking, I wasn't sure how comfortable anyone was going to be speaking candidly with a new CEO. I wanted to create an environment where associates were fully engaged and felt that they had value to add to the culture and the company overall—but how could I be sure I was drawing them out? So I passed around index cards and asked everyone to fill out the cards anonymously, stating what they most wanted me to change and what they didn't want to see change.

The second big objective of all listen-and-learn venues is to demonstrate, and make sure everyone understands, that the company is renewing its commitment, or embarking on a commitment, to justice, equity, diversity, and inclusion. Be honest in these discussions about where the company stands.

And in any format, what's key to a successful outcome is that the leaders do more listening than talking. When you do talk, personalize, using your own life and career experiences. Ask the people who work for you to do the same. If you're a CEO who hasn't spoken candidly in the past, just be clear about what you know and don't know about race, diversity, and inclusion. As business leaders start to realize how critical it is to take a stand in this moment, I've seen many establish the authenticity they need by speaking out and admitting, "I'm on a learning curve."

Of course, a large percentage of CEOs and board members are *not* comfortable having this conversation, and that's completely understandable. We've never had conversations about structural and systemic racism in the workplace before. It's doubly uncomfortable if you're a corporate leader who's always considered it your job to have all the answers. Examining social justice and racism is more about asking questions than providing answers, however, which means that when you're willing to ask questions, you set an excellent example. You show everyone that their CEO and senior managers are working, just as they are, to educate themselves and get better at DEI, taking bolder actions as they learn.

But what questions should a CEO ask to show that they genuinely want to understand what it's like to be powerless or marginalized and how the organization can change things for the better? How do you ask in a way that assures low-level employees that they can trust you to do right by them? How do you lead a conversation about race and inclusion?

Begin with a brief story about what brought you to this room. I always tell my staff about my humble beginnings and how my mother understood my potential, but that same potential wasn't recognized in the same way with employers. If you come from privilege, acknowledge it, then explain how you came to the realization that the company could do a better job of being inclusive.

Then ask some targeted questions, such as:

- Have you ever experienced behavior that seems discriminatory in this workplace?

- How can we make this a better workplace for you?

- What are three things you'd like to see change in this workplace?

At roundtables you can invite the participants to introduce themselves. Introductions will be useful, because often those in attendance will be from cross-functional teams and therefore they won't necessarily know one another. But add value to their introductions by asking each participant to talk about what they're working on and what most excites them about their work—you're trying to get a sense of their passions and their potential.

Let your audience know that you are going to take their comments to heart and come back in several weeks—announce a specific date—with an action plan on how everyone is going to work together on achieving a more inclusive culture. Let them know that the results will not be instant. Typically, it takes two to three years to achieve all of your goals, though you'll set up incremental milestones.

Enlist and Align across the Senior Leadership Team

Every new DEI effort must reach people at multiple levels throughout the organization, and its success will require commitment from everyone. After your listening tour, share the findings with senior management and the board of directors. When a transformation fails, it's often because the buy-in stops at the top level or one level down. Some other high-priority item comes up and the DEI effort takes a back seat, or too many senior leaders are resistant to change, or the CEO doesn't create a system that ensures management will carry out the hard work. In the chapters that follow, I'll discuss what it takes to enlist additional partners from HR and middle management as catalysts for a cultural transformation, but first, you must ensure that from here on, DEI is going to be woven into the fabric of the organization from the top, so that it is not just an isolated initiative but is also part of the way you do business.

Alignment generally starts with making the business case for DEI—and that is something that should be easy with all of the studies over the past decade showing the correlation between diversity and performance. You can remind your managers that diversity allows a company to solve problems more completely and drives innovation in ways that can take you much further. But with the business case established, your role needs to be one of leading a conversation about race and diversity.

I worked with a cohort of a dozen CEOs who belonged to the J.E.D.I. Collaborative for the natural-products industry, helping guide them in making these uncomfortable conversations more palatable to all participants, and any number of creative ideas for breaking down barriers to such discussions emerged. One CEO, Blair Kellison, who heads up the organic tea company Traditional Medicinals, assigned Ijeoma Oluo's *So You Want to Talk about Race* as required reading for his entire management team. He bought a copy of the book for every employee, and then invited author Oluo to speak at a Zoom town hall for the entire company. The straightforward message in Oluo's book served as a kind of leveling tool for conversations. It gave everyone a common set of talking points, ideas, and even language for taking some important actions in the way they hire and promote people.

With these conversations, you give all senior leaders a chance to educate themselves. It is also helpful to bring in external resources, the way Leslie Stretch at Medallia has brought in a diverse group of business leaders, myself included, to talk frankly about their own lived experiences and why businesses thrive when they're inclusive.

From there, you have to let your senior teams know that there will be lucrative incentives for those who carry out an intentional DEI strategy—and consequences for those who don't. A certain percentage of executive bonuses should be tied to meeting a set of goals in this area. Your mandate will be buffered by the increasing possibility that even if you don't push for this, shareholders and other stakeholders will. There's no choice, because good performance increasingly includes deliberate acts to foster diversity and inclusion.

Inevitably, those goals will include more diversity right where you're all sitting: in the executive suites and the boardroom. The more diverse your top ranks are, the more likely the senior teams will be to embrace an intentionally diverse culture. The leadership advisory firm Egon Zehnder, in its annual Global Board Diversity Tracker report for 2020, says it takes at least three underrepresented voices in a boardroom to truly change the internal dynamics. "Rather than seeing one person as the token stand-in, a larger group allows the individuals to be heard for their perspectives rather than for their perceived identity," the report says.[5]

But if you look around the room and pretty much everyone present is white, that brings up one of the biggest challenges of all in this cultural transformation. How do you persuade your white executives and board members to create changes that they might not believe to be in their best interests?

When I started at Jamba and held meetings at which I described the agenda and how we were going to work, I knew I'd encounter a certain amount of resistance. You have to go in knowing that some executives will have a different view on how the company should address racism. Give everyone the opportunity to get engaged and involved—or, if they prefer, they can free up their future.

However, there is always a place at the table for those executives who support the new initiatives with empathy and an eye toward embracing the challenges of a transition. The cultural transformation will take several years, and one of the most important contributions that senior leaders can make is to intentionally begin recruiting, developing, and promoting talent based on new criteria, striving to create a leadership-succession pipeline that looks more like society at large, and in all probability, more like the company's customer base.

Audit the Culture

Auditing is a more formal process for determining how your corporate culture is working for its stakeholders. I think of the audit as a kind of archeological expedition.

You have the known artifacts in the form of written statements: "Our Mission" and "Our Values." Beyond those statements, however, you have to dig to find out how policies are working in practice and how people experience the company. It gives you the current state. It grounds you in facts: policies, people, who has been promoted, the pipeline, how high into the ranks efforts have reached. If you are in the retail or restaurant industry, most likely you've got great diversity in the frontline workforce, but as you move up to middle management, people of color and women taper off. In the restaurant industry, about 49 percent of the frontline workers are people of color, but the farther you go up the hierarchy the whiter and more male representation becomes.[6] Needless to say, systemic factors have created this scenario, and several generations of affirmative action have not created a significant shift. Business leaders are in a good position to change the picture. The audit shows you where the ceiling for advancement begins for certain demographics.

Many companies already use third-party survey firms to conduct pulse surveys and employee-engagement surveys; I've listed a number of these firms in the "Resources for Workplace-Experience Audits and Employee-Engagement Signaling" in the appendix. Third-party auditors can give you a snapshot of how the company looks to your employees, customers, suppliers, and others in the value chain. My colleague, founding director of the Center for WorkLife Law Joan Williams's Workplace Experience Survey identifies basic patterns of racial and gender bias, where they're playing out, and the impact on employees' feelings about belonging and staying with the company. At Jamba Juice I regularly used a version of the Gallup Q^{12} Employee Engagement Survey. This is an audit tool that asks for employee responses to such statements as "I feel that I belong here," "I have the tools to get my job done," "I have a best friend at work," and "My compensation is commensurate with others performing similar jobs." These are critical measurements of whether the respondent feels comfortable in the work environment. You're looking for an assessment of who feels *included*.

Because the survey is kept anonymous, it can ask questions about a person's ethnicity, sexual orientation, gender, age, education, job level, whether they have disabilities, and such. With this data, you break down the responses into segments to determine whether there are noninclusive patterns: Do Black employees feel, in the main, that they are not getting the tools they need to do their jobs effectively? Do women of color at the associate level feel near unanimously that they are being overlooked for the most important assignments? Audit results can show whether there are systemic ways in which some people are being held back, as well as how your company's results compare with those of the industry in general.

I've worked with any number of CEOs who were surprised—sometimes positively, sometimes negatively—by the results of a corporate audit. I always tell them that whatever they learn, it's okay. A large wholesale distribution company, for example, found that of its ten distribution facilities, several had highly inclusive practices—and others didn't. That's what the audit is for: it identifies the blind spots, and then you embark on a corrective course. The distribution company used the findings to start examining the way things were done in the inclusive facilities, and then operationalized its best practices throughout the company.

Some CEOs have chosen to make their change and learning efforts very public, which in itself can be a way of showing that you understand the systemic flaws in society and are going to make your company a high-profile role model that others can follow.

Bracken Darrell, the CEO of the computer-peripheral and software manufacturer Logitech, is one such business leader who took stock of society and his own company and realized he could do much more. In looking at how he could be a more active change agent, he found that he could make a big difference in facilitating the growth of smaller supplier businesses owned by women and people of color by committing to supplier diversity. That led Darrell to issue a public diversity pledge in which he promised to increase the number of suppliers from underrepresented groups across the globe: "We believe our supply base should be reflective of the diversity of the communities and markets that we serve," Darrell said in a company strategy statement.[7]

While it isn't essential for a company to issue a splashy public statement about its efforts to become more inclusive, out-loud reflections such as Darrell's can give other business leaders permission to recognize that none of us is perfect, not one of us has all the answers, yet we can still take the initiative to make improvements in our own organizations that will ultimately encourage others to be part of the solution.

Those CEOs who prefer to keep a lower profile can communicate their intentions internally, although I do recommend making public statements about anything you do that will have an impact on the community, such as training disadvantaged students, distributing food in needy communities, or sponsoring inner-city education or sports programs. That's something Todd Schnuck at Schnuck Markets has started doing, spearheading a number of efforts to support underserved communities in St. Louis and southern Missouri. The most immediate advertisement for the company's stand is a T-shirt that says "Unity is power" on the front and "We stand together against racism" on the back. But to put the message into action, the company has a foundation to address food insecurity and is looking at the best ways to get more food donations into the neighborhoods that need them the most. Schnuck Markets also made a $100,000 investment in fighting education disparities by providing computers and Wi-Fi to disadvantaged students so that they could study from home during the pandemic.

Document What You're Doing Now

Once you have a grasp on how employees and stakeholders perceive the corporate culture and practices and you've gained a sense of what is and isn't working for whom, you can match perception to reality. It's now time to assess all of the existing programs and practices to see what's working well and what needs to improve.

Don't try to judge the findings of your audit; just compile every-thing into a factual "state of the organization." How many white people do you have in your management ranks versus people of color? How many LGBTQIA+ people? Take a hard look at how you hire people. Do you have diverse slates of candidates? Do you mandate a diverse slate? What are the processes for promotion? If you pull out a list of high-potential candidates, how much diversity is in that list? You can bring in third-party resources to audit this process and assess how your company stacks up against the industry as a whole. Document all of your current programs, best practices, and gaps.

Then set a destination and begin making changes to reach it.

I've talked about how Brian Cornell at Target has been vocal about making the company a force for social change. As part of this effort, he has turned to Laysha Ward, who is the company's chief external engagement officer and another ideal executive for this moment. Her role is to strengthen the Target brand with external stakeholders. On the job she runs the Target Foundation, sustainability programs, and community outreach. On a personal level, in early 2020, she told *Black Enterprise* magazine something that echoes exactly what business leaders should be saying now: "I wish I'd learned sooner it's not a sign of weakness to ask for help and that I didn't have to have all the answers. We all get better together."[8]

Target has also documented both its racial and gender breakdown across all levels of the organization and its goals for greater DEI in the future. In a very focused assessment of African American representation, Cornell found the company behind the curve. He issued a public statement revealing that in Target's workforce of nearly 350,000 team members, about half were people of color and 58 percent were women. The percentages declined significantly in the leadership ranks, with 42 percent of Target's leadership team composed of women and 24 percent composed of people of color. Also documented were the positive findings that Target had doubled the representation of company officers of color since 2015 and had a board in which a third of all directors were women and nearly half were Latinx or Black.

Cornell has committed to doing still more, with a goal to increase representation of Black team members across the company by 20 percent by 2023, bringing in a more diverse workforce through a sharper focus on advancement, retention, and hiring.[9] To help meet these goals he's doubled down on programs that include cross-functional mentoring, STEM leadership, development training, and more than one hundred employee resource groups. Performance and compensation evaluations for the top three hundred leaders in the company are closely tied to turnover and DEI metrics.[10]

The poster CEO for how *not* to document your progress in achieving diversity is Charles Scharf at Wells Fargo, who in June 2020 stated in a meeting, and then in a memo to employees that was seen by Reuters, "there is a very limited pool of Black talent to recruit from."[11] Although Scharf was in the process of creating new diversity initiatives, the comment led to widespread backlash when Reuters published the memo in September of that year, and Scharf quickly issued an apology for "making an insensitive comment reflecting my own unconscious bias." His original statement was one that I'm fully aware reflects what a lot of business leaders believe, but it was a case of a leader being underprepared for this moment and less than thoughtful about how to assess what needs to be done.

If Scharf had said in his message: "I'm perplexed; others are doing a better job of this, and we've got to do something more," that would have been an indication that this was a business leader who was starting to recognize that he needed to figure out how to recruit and develop more diverse talent. That kind of proactive stance always goes over better than damage control. You lay out exactly what you've done to achieve a workforce that looks more like society at large, and if your list comes up short, be up-front about it. Then review your recruiting practices and tap into the multiple resources out there that can be of help in broadening your search.

Establish Benchmarks

You've listened. You've brought all of your managers on board, even if that necessitated some changes. You've audited and documented the current state. Now you need to measure progress against benchmarks—not just internal benchmarks of your goals but also measurements that show how your results stack up against those of industry competitors, other businesses in your geographic purview, and society at large. This establishes a way to gauge progress, quarter by quarter and then more exhaustively on an annual basis, quantifying how your company is doing when it comes to recruiting, promotions, retaining, and having a workforce in which everyone feels that they are valued.

Set goals: What do you want the demographics of the company to look like in the future? By when? What is the vision? What hiring practices do you want to put in place? How many people of color do you want to have in senior management, and by when? How many women and people of color do you want to have on the board, by when? How do you want people to experience the company? How are you getting feedback on the organization from your workforce? What are they saying? How are you engaging the community, and how would you like to engage it further? What is your action plan to change the metrics? Then keep score of the progress (see table 3-1).

TABLE 3-1

Benchmarks to measure

	Q1	Q2	Q3	YTD	Target

Employee value proposition

1. I feel like I belong.

2. I see myself growing here.

3. I trust my manager.

4. I have leaders who care about my well-being.

Employee engagement

1. I would recommend this company to family and friends.

2. I see myself growing here.

3. I would like to be working here one year from now.

4. I am willing to give extra effort to ensure my customers (clients) have a great experience.

5. My work is meaningful.

Retention

1. Retention of general managers

2. Retention of director and above

3. Retention of key talent

Diversity measurement examples

1. Corporate officers: women

2. Corporate officers: people of color, disaggregated by race

3. Director and above: women

4. Director and above: people of color, disaggregated by race

5. Director and above, new hires: women

6. Director and above, new hires: people of color, disaggregated by race

Some companies have formed working groups to monitor their benchmarks so that the companies can continue to hold themselves accountable over the long term. Schnuck Markets, for example, holds weekly meetings, and then I, as a board member, meet with the working group once a month. In those gatherings we review our progress in meeting targets and refine our approach accordingly.

Build Action-Learning Teams or Task Forces

Professor Reginald Revans pioneered the concept of action learning in the 1940s, when he was working with managers of the UK Coal Board, and since then it's been used in myriad ways in the business world. Basically, it's a process that involves a small group working on real problems, taking action, and learning as individuals, as a team, and as an organization. It helps organizations develop creative, flexible, and successful strategies for dealing with pressing problems.[12] Throughout my career, I've found that setting up action-learning teams is the most inclusive way to help catalyze an agenda, solve problems, reshape culture, and answer strategic challenges. If the problem you're addressing is the need to meet the goals and measure up to the benchmarks you've established as necessary for a more diverse and inclusive culture, consider setting up action-learning teams, a time-tested way to ensure the best foundation for a transformation. The directive comes from the top, but diverse voices are actively engaged in building the future.

What is action learning, after all, if not a way to teach others to become leaders, thinking critically and working collaboratively?

Because the team's whole purpose is to work together to innovate and solve previously intractable problems, the members are likely to be bolder about proposing unheard-of big ideas than they might be if they were flying solo.

Two of the world's best-known proponents of action learning were Jack Welch and Roger Enrico. In *The Leadership Engine*, Noel Tichy outlines how both CEOs taught others to lead by teaching them to take on real challenges and own the outcomes. As CEO of PepsiCo, Enrico would lead nine executives at a time through five days of action learning. He would tell them about his own experiences in the business and coach them on their personal operating styles. He had each participant take on a "grow the business" project that would have a significant dollar impact on the company. He would coach them on the objectives and implementation and then send them out to work on their projects, returning several months later to review their progress. Welch, when he was CEO at GE, taught leadership every couple of weeks at GE's Crotonville management development center. One of the questions he would ask participants in the most senior program was, "If you were named CEO of GE tomorrow, what would you do?" He used the question "to orchestrate a no-holds-barred discussion in which he jousted with participants and honed their analytic abilities and leadership instincts by having them also joust with each other."[13]

The problem-solving groups start with a team, task force, or work group of fifteen to twenty people whom the CEO handpicks, with breakout groups of five to eight people. The group comprises managers from various levels. When your goal is transforming your corporate culture into one that fully embraces DEI, it's helpful to instruct the action teams to think big in this way. At Jamba Juice I made the teams diverse by design, choosing previously overlooked employees for the ALTs. If you do this, your action-learning teams are likely to be far more diverse than the company's workforce as a whole.

I've found that the most effective ALTs always include strong representation from middle management. You can't make the track to promotions more diverse unless you have middle managers as part of the effort; they're the key to breaking systemic barriers.[14] Why? Middle managers are typically the ones who control who get the high-profile assignments that put junior-level people into the pipeline for greater responsibilities, and the bias of middle managers can go a long way in explaining why many diversity initiatives fail. In an organization of 100,000 people, you might have no more than 150 people controlling the work experiences of everyone else. At every organization I've helped lead, I've found that you need effective policies to embed diversity and inclusion into the DNA, but middle-level managers hold the key to delivering it. (In chapter 4, I'll talk in more detail about how to enlist middle managers as catalysts for transformation.)

The action teams will work closely with the CEO and other leaders, such as the chief human resources officer (CHRO), functioning as the steering committee for the change effort. Typically, the assignment will take place over a period of sixty to ninety days, though I've seen groups achieve objectives in as few as thirty to forty-five days. The team members should meet once a week to examine the issue, to determine the objectives and the priorities for reaching those objectives, and to make recommendations. Typically, the teams should have no more than one or two critical items to examine. They should take on specific challenges, with a time frame to deliver recommendations on one or two granular questions. A clear agenda, a specific timeline, and some minimum threshold of deliverables will produce stronger, more-effective innovation. I've found that ALTs will almost always exceed your expectations as long as they have a clear assignment and clear parameters, with clearly spelled-out processes, check-ins, milestones, and deadlines.

At Jamba Juice we used action-learning teams to study several growth initiatives. One team took on the question, How should we expand internationally? Another looked at the question, How will we get Jamba Juice stands into more airports? Another figured out how to make significant changes to the menus at the franchised restaurants in a couple of months. Previously, changing menus was an eighteen-month project. I was looking for faster innovation—and all of my teams, by design, were highly diverse in terms of work experience, background, ethnicity, and gender. Mike Fuccillo, who was my director of marketing and communications at Jamba and who headed up about ten different ALTs during my time there, now tells me that the head of the design team came into his office shrieking about having to change the menus so quickly.

"But then he saw that he could do it," Fuccillo recalls. "It was all about taking out the fear factor and getting everyone on board to just get things done."[15]

These days I often advise companies about setting up diverse ALTs to study diversity itself and to help speed up the development of their

DEI initiatives—and I'm always stressing that point about the fear factor and how a group of diverse minds can eliminate the fear of doing things differently.

I'm now serving on the board of the Bay Club Company, which operates luxury sports and fitness resorts all over the West Coast, and helping advise its action-learning program. The CEO, Matthew Stevens, launched a diversity task force in the summer of 2020, and since then company leaders in four locations have formed teams that are deploying action-learning principles to answer the following question: How can we create an inclusive environment where individuals of all backgrounds are celebrated and can thrive? They've come up with multiple actions. They've created a video for all employees discussing why an inclusive environment is important, conducted an education series, had task-force members lead safe-space fireside chats with employees, and started a cultural-celebration space in their monthly newsletter, highlighting employees' ethnic backgrounds. The latter, says Stevens, is a way of "learning more about the things that make us different and the things that bring us together at the same time."[16]

Develop an Action Plan

You've promised your employees that you'd have a plan ready by a certain date. This is the action plan. Factoring in all that you've learned from your listen-and-learn sessions, management meetings, surveys, and audits, and from the ongoing education everyone is getting from discussions about race, organizational climate, and belonging, it's now time to draw up a thoughtful, comprehensive blueprint showing how you will incorporate changes into the organizational culture over the next several years.

Set goals for each quarter of the year ahead. In the first quarter, you should launch an executive diversity council. This group should include the CEO, the head of HR, the chief diversity officer and others on the diversity-and-inclusion teams, and leaders from key business units or divisions of the company.

Other goals for the first year might look something like this:

Q1

Develop a community-engagement initiative.

Increase supplier diversity.

Launch a communication initiative to let all employees know about your plans to hire and promote more people from underrepresented groups.

Q2

Launch a DEI council with specific roles, responsibilities, and deliverables.

Q3

Form employee resource groups for Black/African American, Latinx, and LGBTQIA+ associates.

Q4

Begin a comprehensive DEI training program.

Develop a strategy and targets to evaluate and support supplier diversity over the long term.

These are examples, but every company's action plan will be tailored to the company's most pressing needs.

The action plan should also spell out longer-term commitments for the next two to three years. This is where you can set specific representation goals. You might state, as Target and Starbucks have, that you will:

- increase the number of Black and Latinx senior managers by a certain percentage by a certain year;

- increase the representation of Black, female, and LGBTQIA+ board members by a certain percentage the year after that.

The action plan is something you can circulate throughout the company, stating the basic goals so that every employee at every level is aware that you're building an intentional culture step by step. You should, of course, plan to hold more town halls and smaller meetings over the next few years, as well as send out newsletters or messages through the internal website, letting everyone know how the company is doing when it comes to meeting the goals set in the action plan. That will be an ongoing challenge, but the goals will be a natural extension of your business strategies if you build a design for change throughout the organization—a plan that I'll explain in chapter 4.

Key Takeaway

Start talking openly about race and systemic racism in the corporate world, and then start changing the systems and structures.

Checklist for CEOs

✓ Call a series of town-hall meetings that include the entire workforce.

✓ Organize roundtable discussions with smaller groups of managers.

✓ Discuss the transformation with all executive leaders to be sure the senior teams are aligned.

✓ Conduct an audit of the culture.

✓ Tabulate the results and identify the problem areas.

✓ Document what you're doing now and what needs to be accomplished.

✓ Establish benchmarks and goals with time frames.

✓ Set up action-learning teams to enable the work.

✓ Develop cross-functional dialogue.

✓ Establish an action plan and road map.

Transforming the Culture by Design

The murder of George Floyd hit too close to home for Leslie Stretch, the CEO of Medallia. He is a white man from Scotland married to a wife of Nigerian descent—and as with Lisa Wardell, then at Adtalem, the news made him think of his own children. He's had to talk with his kids about what to do if the police ever stop them. And in June 2020, as he watched the news about Black Lives Matter demonstrations all around the country, he realized that as the head of a $6 billion technology company, he was in a position to make his company more of a model for society, tackling systemic racism in America by ensuring that the representation of Black and brown professionals in his company was more reflective of society as a whole. In a letter to his staff that remains on the Medallia website, he wrote, "The 2019 Census records the US population as 13% Black or African American. We are miles from this with only 1% of our US employees self-identified as Black or African American. We can do better."[1]

Then he designed a plan for change. Part of the plan is to bring more Black people into the technology industry; in an email that went out to all staff in June 2020 he stated that he wanted the company to increase its Black representation from only 1 percent at the time to 3 percent by February 15, 2021; 6 percent by February 15, 2022; and 13 percent by February 15, 2023. As an incentive, his plan puts 100 percent of the executive teams' bonuses at risk; leaders will not receive equity award refresh grants unless these goals are achieved each year. He has directed executives and HR leaders to actively seek Black candidates, especially for roles where the Black presence has been consistently low, such as sales and engineering, and has committed to recruiting through career fairs like AfroTech and through historically Black colleges and universities.

Beyond hiring, Stretch is driving a message about what the company stands for. Juneteenth is now an annual holiday. He is inviting external speakers—I have been one of them—to talk to employees and management about how the business world looks when you're Black, or Hispanic, or LGBTQIA+, or female. "The recurring nature of these measures are very important to attempt to break the cycle of ignorance and inequality," Stretch said in his email to the staff.

I've talked with Stretch at length about how he came to see anti-racism as a motivating factor in his life and his business. He recalls his own upbringing in Scotland, and how important it was to have a boss who recognized his potential. At sixteen, he got a job as an elevator operator and security guard at Goldberg's, a family-owned department store in Edinburgh, an hour and a half by bus from his home. "After my first day, I said I can't do it, the commute was too exhausting," he recalls. "So I phoned my boss and said I quit. Most people would have said, 'Okay, you're done.'" But his boss said, "Take a day off, then come in late next week and at five o'clock we'll go to a pub and have a pint. If you decide you're finished after that, that's fine." As Stretch sees it, this was a manager who changed his life, because he listened to Stretch with empathy and didn't give up on him. Stretch stayed with the department store for eight years, working part-time while he was at university and graduate school, and left with enough money to buy a computer, learn to code, and get into the technology business.

In his studies, he became fascinated with the history of the American Civil War and Abraham Lincoln's words that "a house divided against itself cannot stand." In 1986, when thirty-two nations boycotted the Commonwealth Games in Edinburgh over the UK government's support of trade with apartheid-era South Africa, and over inclusion of two South African–born athletes on the England team, Stretch thought of the "house divided" concept and joined the anti-apartheid demonstrations.

"In America, it still feels like a house divided," he says. "From a business perspective, if you're tapping into only 25 percent of the talent quotient, you're missing out."

He says that the biggest change he's seen since Black Lives Matter gained steam in 2020 is "you can't say it's got nothing to do with us. A business is a microcosm of society. You can't just say all the right words and hope it will go away."

He believes it has been important to put money on the table to fight racism, because money incentivizes everyone—and is therefore an investment in the future. "Prosperity and success depend on social stability, and in my view, equality and diversity," he says. "The future of free enterprise depends on this, so you should be all-in."

Stretch is building an anti-racist, diverse culture, and the way he's doing it is instructional. It's something you build intentionally, by design, with a blueprint that everyone in your organization can follow—and he has found that the effort pays off in all kinds of ways. "The talent you'll find, the education you'll receive from your team as you embrace this, is one of the most fulfilling things you'll ever experience," he says. "There is only upside."[2]

I've said that DEI needs to come from the top, and that today, with the conversation around race, racism, and building anti-racist organizations, you need to be a leader who doesn't shy away from talking openly about race and systemic racism. Here are two more principles for building the kind of intentional culture of diversity that meets the needs of business today:

- Integrate diversity and inclusion into everything you do and say as a business leader.

- Make diversity and inclusion an engine of your business performance.

In chapter 3, I talked about the action plan, which is a concrete road map for achieving your DEI goals. Designing for change through the above principles is something bigger and more philosophical. It's your worldview, and your approach to making DEI an engine of your business strategy. It's the way you will let all of your stakeholders know that it's an essential part of the way you do business.

By design, you will intentionally interrupt all of the systems in your company that undermine diversity and inclusion, deploying in their stead the tools to create a culture of diversity and inclusion. You will be changing deeply ingrained practices and habits in such areas as hiring, performance reviews, promotions, succession planning, and key project assignments. That will mean a shift in what is expected of leaders at every level; they will be required to help create an environment in which no one's talents and potential are overlooked. None of this will be easy or instantaneous. To instill a change in mindset, and scale that change throughout the organization, it's imperative that everyone knows *why* you're doing this.

Part of the answer is that systemic and structural barriers to diversity and inclusion are real, and companies need to be proactive in dismantling these barriers. No business wants to be exposed and subject to lawsuits the way Tyson Foods was in 2020. The meatpacking industry had already displayed a gross lack of concern for the safety of its workers—many of them Black and brown—as Covid-19 spread through its processing plants. Then came the news that supervisors at an Iowa Tyson Foods plant had placed bets on how many workers would become infected with coronavirus, demonstrating "wanton disregard for worker safety" as a wrongful-death lawsuit alleged.[3]

After the fact, Tyson fired seven plant managers and launched its own investigation into their behavior. It also instituted safety measures against the spread of coronavirus, albeit after ten thousand employees had tested positive. But all of this is a distraction from running and growing a business, which is a way of saying that a discriminatory culture creates financial and reputational risks that are avoidable with more-thoughtful leadership.

On the flip side, we've been hearing for years that proactive DEI leads to essential outcomes such as growth, innovation, and better employee morale. But what we're now seeing in the world's most valuable companies is something that goes further. DEI is *an important part of what drives the business.* To be sustainable, it must play a major role in business performance; if it doesn't, your busy executives have an excuse for losing interest. That's why I've always viewed building a diverse and inclusive organization as a business and *strategic* imperative.

Think of how you would scale other organizational transformations so that they became integrated into the everyday fabric—say, absorbing a large acquisition, overhauling product lines, or implementing digital technology. Broadly speaking, there are four main parts to the design for change:

1. Use action-learning principles and employee resource groups to drive business outcomes.

2. Create a highly intentional communication strategy.

3. Enlist key leaders as catalysts for change.

4. Reimagine and redesign your "people" strategy.

We can use this same blueprint to transform the culture by design. Let's look at each element and how they can work to build change into the organization.

Use Action-Learning Principles and Employee Resource Groups to Drive Business Outcomes

The way I've used action learning has been mostly through teams that I handpick and assign a problem to solve. However, it's a concept that applies to any situation in which you present a challenge and assign a group of people to examine ideas and help build a plan for achieving the desired future state. When you want to build in DEI as a way of doing business, there is no better tool than action learning to make diversity and inclusion a natural part of your strategy. You bring in people from diverse backgrounds and cross-functions to brainstorm and have each person in the room discuss the challenge and the potential solutions from their particular perspective. That way everyone is forced to consider ideas outside their own lens. I've seen people who previously may not have been comfortable speaking up have a chance to shine. Action learning is designed to ensure that every participant thinks critically and works collaboratively, thereby developing their leadership skills. So you can use it to help build a more diverse pipeline of candidates for promotion while at the same time gaining a wider frame of reference when it comes to generating business ideas.

Here are some business goals you can achieve by using action-learning principles:

Grow new markets

When I joined Gillette in 2002, Jim Kilts was the chairman and CEO. He had come from Nabisco, which was a far more diverse consumer-products company, and he wanted Gillette to catch up, creating a company that was more reflective of evolving consumer markets. We found that an intentional program of supplier diversity was an immediate way of bringing in new voices. To that end, we added our first African American—and Latinx-owned marketing agencies, Fuse Advertising and LatinWorks, respectively, in an initiative that was led by Julie

Washington, at the time the vice present of commercial marketing. The result was a more thoughtful approach to our multicultural consumers from an advertising, messaging, and product perspective.

Take the shaving category. Through our new agencies, we reached out to Black and Latinx customers and found that existing ad campaigns weren't speaking to this market. Black men tend to get razor bumps from shaving, and we presented research showing that there was a whole overlooked market of men who would happily buy a gentler shaver that would cause less discomfort. So we developed a new kind of razor and a marketing campaign for it.

Make DEI a business unit

Another excellent example of what happens when you make DEI an intentional business strategy is the work that Clorox has done. It is not by accident that, at this writing, the CEO is a woman, Linda Rendle, while the executive team has Asian and African American representation. Over the past fifteen years, the Clorox Company has been developing a culture of inclusion that is instructional to any business leader seeking to scale DEI throughout the organization.

In 2006 Donald Knauss became CEO (a job he held until 2014) and hired Erby Foster to be Clorox's chief diversity officer. At the time it was a job they both knew would have to be invented from scratch, but Knauss liked Foster's idea that DEI should be a business imperative rather than just a social-justice issue. Foster ran his DEI division as a business unit. Much of what he did there involved building diverse teams through employee resource groups (ERGs) that functioned in many ways as action-learning teams.

What Foster created was an ideal template for the role of a chief diversity officer. Because the CEO has to be steering the strategy, and may have to delegate the day-to-day DEI effort to a CDO, that CDO should be someone who will run the operation as a visionary leader, with the goal of using diversity and inclusion to create a competitive advantage.

"The way I describe it is I created pull, not push," says Foster, who started out as one of a handful of Black CPAs at Arthur Andersen and became a DEI expert not by design, but because he saw a crying need to open doors for Black professionals. He now runs a consulting firm for companies seeking cultural transformation, Foster Inclusion.

"Push," he explains, "is if you have a government contract and they say you have to comply with affirmative-action criteria. So the government pushes me, the CDO, and I push the company. People will comply but eventually push back. They'll say they're too busy running the business to attend diversity meetings. You'll be left with nothing but activities. You might celebrate Black History Month, but you won't make real changes."[4]

What he did instead was start pulling people into ERGs. These he saw as serving a multifold purpose—not just the traditional role of advocating for their members and helping them develop skills, but also functioning as business teams. The first big success story came from the Asian ERG in 2010. Foster had done research and found that, in the United States alone, Asian consumers had $600 billion in annual buying power. "This was a market we weren't talking to," he says. So CEO Knauss addressed the members of the ERG and asked them to come up with ideas for targeting the Asian market. It was a rather typical CEO action-learning briefing, reminiscent of the way

Jack Welch would address a group of executives at GE, spending about an hour discussing a challenge he wanted them to take on, and telling them to come back in thirty days with a plan.

At Clorox, the ERG members had six months, and within that time they came up with three big business ideas: taking Clorox home-cleaning products to India, marketing the Green Works line of biodegradable cleaning products to the Asian market, and acquiring a small specialty-food company. For the third idea, the group had a list of ten potential acquisition targets. The company followed up, and the next year Clorox bought Soy Vay Enterprises, of Felton, California, a manufacturer of kosher Asian sauces, salad dressings, and condiments.[5] It was the 100-year-old Clorox Company's first entry into the food sector, but with this new set of data and insights into the buying power and habits of Asian consumers, the company had a business case for expanding its product lines further—something that happened again and again once Foster decided that a little competition among ERGs would lead to more big ideas.

As he puts it: "I went to the Latinx group and told them 'the Asian group is kicking your butts.'"

That fired up the Latinx Employee Resource Group (Latinx ERG), and the members launched their own business studies. They noted that millennial Latinos love the flavors they grew up with but are unlikely to spend the time required to cook traditional dishes, so they came up with a proposal to expand the food portfolio, resulting in Clorox's acquisition of Nueva Cocina, a maker of Latin rice, seasoning, and soup mixes that was started by two Cuban women in Miami.

Clorox now boasts a number of business initiatives that originated with employee resource groups. Pride, the company's LGBTQIA+

group, was the main force behind such marketing efforts as the Burt's Bees Rainbow Pride Lip Balm Pack and the Fresh Step cat-litter advertising campaign targeted to gay men. The group found demographic research indicating that gay men were more likely than most other American households to have cats—but that isn't a statistic most companies take into account unless a diverse pool of employees is encouraged to share what it knows from its members' own life experiences. Similarly, Clorox's African Americans Building Leadership Excellence (ABLE) ERG has helped the company develop a stronger foothold in the Black consumer market through such initiatives as a partnership between Kingsford charcoal and *Ebony* magazine for a summer-grilling campaign, and advertisements for Glad and Pine-Sol that target Black consumers.

Identify a more diverse pipeline of people with potential

Here's another way that ERGs can serve as a business unit: they can provide an answer to the evaluation gap that was so ever-present in my early career. I'm talking about how senior management spots "potential," and how no one ever promoted me based on potential. Rather, I had to basically perform the duties required at the next rung to prove that I was promotable after the fact.

But what if you charge ERGs with the responsibility of selecting individuals with high potential from within the group? That's exactly what Dr. Deborah Ashton has done. Ashton has a PhD in clinical psychology from Harvard but spent much of her career heading up the DEI work at large companies, including Darden Restaurants, Harley-Davidson,

Medtronic, and Novant Health before starting her own DEI consulting firm, Planet Perspective. "We found plenty of high-potential women and people of color by having the ERGs nominate them," she says. "Then they got the mentoring and sponsoring they needed."[6]

In these cases, the ERGs have deployed the principles of action learning—cross-disciplinary brainstorming, dissecting the problem, and attacking it with outside-the-box solutions—to product and market development as well as to diversity itself. If you pool a group of people with a diversity of expertise and experience, you never know what monumental ideas might emerge.

Create a Highly Intentional Communication Strategy

You've probably noticed that I use the term *systemic racism* throughout this book. That's intentional, to make it clear that I'm talking about overcoming discrimination that was at the foundation of American culture—indeed, it was embedded in American laws and institutions until the enactment of antidiscrimination laws that began in the 1970s. If all I talked about was achieving diversity, that would be a different book with different goals. Here we're talking about going further, to build anti-racist companies and to dismantle biases at every level.

What you say as an organizational leader carries weight, so be very deliberate in your choice of words, as I am here. And in creating a communication strategy for a cultural transformation, I'm talking about something that goes much deeper than just your corporate-communications and marketing messages, though these messages absolutely need to be a reflection of all that you're doing to champion a multicultural society in which everyone can be their authentic selves and live up to their full potential.

A corporate culture is a shared language, and it's reinforced by symbols, rituals, and rewards. An intentional communication strategy means that you support the culture you're building through everything you say and do as the leader, through the way people within the company interact with one another, and through all of the internal and external messages that come from the company.

Speak out when you see bias

Lisa Wardell was one of the most thoughtful CEOs out there when it came to the intentional culture she created at Adtalem—a culture of diversity and inclusion in which she was open about what the company achieved (a highly diverse board, for one thing) and what it still needed to do (she would like to have had more people of color in the executive ranks).

She also made a point of telling people when they're demonstrating bias, although she was judicious in picking her battles. "When you're the CEO, the way you use your time and energy sets an example for everyone," she said. "I try to pick and choose when I speak out so that it's not coming off as judgmental. But I think it's important to let people know when they're seeing something through their own lens and not considering how it might look to others."

The question of how things looked through her lens versus that of a white supplier came up shortly after she became CEO, in a meeting with a marketing firm. It was a woman-owned firm—in fact, the founder was the mother of the man who led the presentation.

"He pulled up a photo of all the employees and said he wanted to show us how diverse the company was," says Wardell. "He was so proud because maybe 80 percent of the people in the picture were women. What I saw, though, was a picture of 100 percent white people. I'm a woman, but that's not my first lens. So I said to him, 'That's wonderful, but let me tell you what I see when I look at this picture.' My team members' mouths were hanging open; they weren't used to my way yet."[7]

Nor was the supplier. I wasn't in the room, but like Wardell, I have become used to seeing stunned faces when I speak from my lived experience. Many people don't see what's happening from the perspective of others until someone tells them and helps broaden their lens.

Design skills for engagement

In any large group, honest communication is difficult. And any two individuals might disagree in the course of doing business together, even in the most homogenous groups. Dissent can be especially counterproductive in a diverse group where people can't fall back on lived experiences, mutually understood codes of behavior, or golf-club memberships and school ties to establish something in common. As I've said, diversity is messy up front. To build a culture in which you can have constructive dialogue between people who don't necessarily see eye-to-eye, I always use a template for engagement and communication that we put to work at Ralston Purina when Nestlé acquired the company.

We used action-learning teams and communication tools to integrate two very different cultures. It wasn't a diversity strategy per se—though it helped us build an intentionally inclusive and collaborative organization—but Janice Duis, a leadership- and organization-development specialist who put the program together for Ralston Purina, continues to use these communication techniques to help scale DEI transformations. I've used the techniques too, in setting up a framework to talk about racism and diversity and how we're going to work together. The language you use will differ from one organization to another, but the point is to create a way of communicating messages and symbols that have the same meaning to everyone within the company.

Duis has designed a toolkit for what she calls "skills for engagement." She often begins the work with a program that teaches participants to conduct dialogue that fuels advocacy and inquiry to create mutual learning. Many of these tools are adapted from *The Fifth Discipline,* the classic book by system scientist and founder of the Society for Organizational Learning Peter Senge that describes how to adopt the strategies of learning organizations, which continuously discover new ways of thinking and creating desirable results. At Ralston Purina, this was a two-day program that everyone in the organization was required to attend.

"It's about understanding another person's perspectives," says Duis of the program. "I form an opinion about someone and need to use inquiry to find out their position." Part of the objective is to break down what she calls a "ladder of inference"—that is, preconceived notions about people that in some cases might be considered biases.[8]

Here's how the ladder of inference works:

- We all have a reflexive loop in our brain.

- We take actions based on our beliefs.

- We draw conclusions, make assumptions.

- We add on meanings that are both cultural and personal.

- We select "data" in our minds that supports what we believe.

Duis's objective is to create discussions with others in which we use inquiry and listen to others' views, thereby challenging our ladder of inference.

At Ralston Purina, executives tended to have the perspective that it was their own experienced people who knew best—yet when they participated in the inquiry sessions and listened to what those from Nestlé had to say, they discovered that many of the newcomers to the merged entity of Nestlé Purina, though they lacked experience in the pet-food industry, had brilliant ideas. We also assigned seemingly incompatible people to work on business projects together. A senior marketing executive who had previously been my rival when we were both at Purina became one of my best friends because we were paired together and had to understand each other's lived experiences and approach to business. Marketing requires a methodical, linear approach. I was in sales, where I had to make what looked like quick, day-to-day decisions as I worked with my customers. In talking it out, I learned that, in her ladder of inference, I looked unprepared. What she didn't know was how much research I would do before I met with clients so that I could arrive at decisions that looked spontaneous. When we were assigned to work together, we learned to show each other how we each approached our work, so that we learned from each other. This cross-functional approach works equally well when your aim is to scale a cultural transformation. You put together people who have clashing strengths and weaknesses so that each has skills to teach the other, but you also create intentional pairings of people who might clash culturally, and you give them the tools to learn more about each other through inquiry.

Duis's third tool for building more-powerful and -productive conversations is something she calls the "left-hand column." It's essentially a way of creating a safe space to share thoughts we wouldn't otherwise feel comfortable expressing in a work setting. At Purina, any of us who had been through the training knew that we could say to a colleague, "I'm speaking from the left-hand column," and our colleague would know that they were going to hear just what we were really thinking.

We learned to apply reasonable filters but still use the left-hand column to express our biggest concerns and get constructive feedback. In using this technique as a tool for enhancing inclusiveness, you have to set boundaries on the purpose. It isn't a license for people to express their biases—rather, it's a way of talking to coworkers about both personal reactions to the workplace and business problems.

As Duis presents it, someone might be thinking, "We can't deliver the project in two weeks—it isn't possible in that time frame," but might also be thinking that if they say that, they'll come across as incompetent. This is the kind of issue that can be a particular burden to minority employees, who feel they have to prove themselves at every step. But what if the employee is able to tell her boss, "Speaking from the left-hand column, I'm concerned that it won't be possible to do a thorough job by that deadline." That opens the way to dialogue that will help head off a supervisor harboring a bias that this is someone who doesn't deliver what she promises.

Bernard Tyson, the late, great former CEO of Kaiser Permanente, had his own way of letting people in the organization speak their minds. His code term was "freedom of speech." He had a standing joke with his senior managers that if they wanted to disagree with him on an issue, they'd ask, "freedom of speech?" he'd say yes, and they'd tell him what they thought. "It's about creating a culture where a nurse can walk in and say, 'I've been thinking about something. What if we did this process 1, 2, 4, 3 instead of 1, 2, 3, 4?'" Tyson said in an interview with *MIT Sloan Management Review.* And he did listen when nurses proposed new ways of doing things. For example, from a suggestion that came from the front lines, nurses began sharing essential patient information during shift changes in the patients' rooms instead of the nurses' stations, so that patients had a voice in their own care.[9]

Some of us have been using these collaborative skills since well before the era of anti-racist leadership, but now it's more important than ever to have a framework that allows you to have courageous but sometimes uncomfortable conversations. Think of it as an essential system for running your business. I'm seeing the Bay Club Company, as one example, encourage employees to talk about their experiences with racism through a system designed by Lloyd and Amber Cook, the company's husband-and-wife DEI director team. They're calling it "the coffee chats." Employees from across the company are invited to come together once a month, sometimes in person and sometimes virtually, in a safe space led by members of a DEI task force that's been set up, to talk about experiences and things they've learned in the workplace and in their lives.

The cloud communication company Twilio has started a video platform called "Did You Know?" which encourages employees to discuss inclusion issues. An episode about the "model minority myth" that gets applied to Asians, for example, featured three employees explaining why a stereotype that some people might see as positive actually upholds white supremacy. As one speaker said, the myth minimizes actual racial discrimination against Asians, and "it implies that hard work and family values can overcome over two centuries of Black enslavement."[10]

Create intentional symbols and artifacts

Visual communication is massively powerful. Be highly intentional in determining the images that employees, customers, suppliers, investors, and society—all stakeholders, in short—are going to identify as representative of what this company produces and what it stands for. What people see when they enter the lobby is more than just window dressing; it reveals the formal culture. I've often talked with Duis about this aspect of inclusiveness, and she says it's especially problematic if no one pays attention to decor that's dated.

"Think about what new hires see when they come through the front door," she says. "Do they see a series of portraits of every former CEO and they're all white males? How am I welcoming people into the organization? Do they see what the company is most recognized for? If you're trying to build a diverse organization, do people of color come in and see others who look like them?"

I once spoke on a panel at which other participants talked about their company bringing in its first African American executive. He told them that as he walked through the halls, he could spot the lack of diversity just in the way the company laid out the product design. No one had thought about how the product photos showed only white people.

Look to the future in the way you showcase the company. And although it might seem paradoxical, connecting with the company's past is also a way of keeping the culture moving forward. Staff and other stakeholders like to know that the present-day CEO's vision is a continuation of the best of the founding ideals.

Several years into my tenure at Jamba, I invited Kirk Perron, the founder, to come back as a consultant, because I knew he was passionate about what the company stood for. He wanted Jamba to be a fun experience for customers, a place that inspired healthy living. In rebuilding the culture, that message became a touchstone that helped us recruit the diverse and impassioned workforce that we needed. Tell the founders' stories to showcase what they did that was courageous and innovative, and how you are carrying on the tradition with a company that you're rebuilding for the world we live in today.

These days, I'm pleased to see a number of companies starting new traditions that point to a more equitable future. One of the most powerful examples is Schnuck Markets. When you walk into any one of the company's supermarkets, you will find the managers, the cashiers, and the people stocking shelves all wearing the company's T-shirt that says, "Unity is power" on the front and "We stand together against racism" on the back. Could there be a clearer statement about what this company stands for?

Enlist Key Leaders as Catalysts for Change

When my colleague, professor and founding director of the Center for WorkLife Law Joan Williams, and I examined what it takes to dismantle structural racism, we found that there are three particular systems that have to be changed. The first two are informal assignment systems and incentive systems, which in most companies are in the hands of middle-level managers. The third, the HR systems, develop a certain approach to recruiting and hiring that, if systemic racism and unconscious bias have been a part of the culture, will transmit racial and gender bias year after year.[11] Through my experiences, and particularly my work at Jamba Juice, I've realized that my direct reports, human resources leaders, and middle management are instrumental in creating organizationwide, sustainable change.

Although the individual managers and HR people who work for your organization might have the best of intentions, they know that they're rewarded for making decisions that reflect the company's values. If those values tend to embrace the hiring and promotion of white males with unlimited "potential," managers throughout the organizational structure will develop an almost intuitive understanding of that. If people in senior management have acted with unconscious bias, for example by frequently judging job candidates who happen to be people of color, women, or members of the LGBTQIA+ community as "not a good fit" for one reason or another, rest assured that everyone will absorb the unspoken message by osmosis. You can't deliver the cultural changes that you need throughout the organization unless you enlist key leaders and make them catalysts for change.

Handpick a group of critical leaders in HR and a diverse group of middle managers and call them into a series of meetings. You might start by discussing what you've learned from your listening sessions and culture audits, and then present the benchmarks you've established and goals you've set. I've seen companies start their diversity initiatives with more antibias training, but tactical training without a strategic plan doesn't change the system. It isn't enough to say we're all aware of systemic racism and want to ensure that our employees of color feel safe at work; people will walk out of those sessions wondering what they're actually supposed to do about the problem. Instead, get your catalyst teams excited about the big vision and their key role in it.

Throughout the meetings, set an example of what empathy looks like. Talk about your personal stake in overcoming racism and creating a more inclusive culture. Maybe you came from a privileged background but witnessed discrimination early on and have never forgotten it. Maybe, like the venture-capitalist friend I mentioned in chapter 1, you have a child who wants to know why people of color get stopped by the police for minor infractions or for no reason at all and end up dead. Maybe, like Lisa Wardell, formerly at Adtalem, you have Black sons and you fear for their safety every time they leave the house. Maybe you just know it's where your business has to go to stay competitive in an increasingly multicultural world.

I have found that the best way to help people see the flaws in their own biases is through continuous dialogue. You can talk at these meetings about your own experiences with flawed assumptions. You can stress how, when two people in the organization seem to be working at cross-purposes, whether because of personal views or cultural differences, they just might learn something from each other if they engage in dialogue and really listen to each other. All of this will be a way of helping your most important catalysts for change sharpen their empathy skills.

Once you've talked about bias, race, racism, and empathy, however, it's time to paint a picture of what inclusive leadership looks like. You should talk about the company's values, and how leaders are expected to treat their staffs. The idea is to unlock the system. Unlock a common language and set of values so that people from different backgrounds can have constructive dialogue even if they don't see eye-to-eye on everything. At Jamba Juice I trained hundreds of people as catalysts for change. What I stressed was that we have a culture of learning; we encourage everyone to ask questions and listen to others, so that we always act with empathy when we're working with others.

Hand off the company's action plan, discussing the goals and the timetable for reaching them as well as the strategies. Share your expectations for the role this team of catalysts will play, and how they will be helping lead the effort. And—critically—let them know that, as the company's key catalysts for transformation, they're preparing to be the leaders of tomorrow. They'll be scaling the cultural change throughout the organization in ways that I'll discuss in detail in chapter 5. They're going to be your elite corps of great leaders.

Reimagine and Redesign Your "People" Strategy

"People" is the name a number of companies have assigned to what used to be known as human resources, but I think of it more as a blanket term for what HR's mission should be. HR should be the part of the company that develops people—in all their diversity of experiences, identities, and skills—as a valuable resource. Sadly, HR has lost this mandate in many companies. At its worst, HR sees humans as a liability; its main functions become identifying where to downsize and delivering the bad news, as well as trying to silence employee complaints about harassment or discrimination. At most companies HR falls somewhere in between, grappling between a desire to do right by employees and the very real need for compliance and legalities. For a company to make sustainable change, the functions of HR must reflect the fact that people are the organization's most important resource. This is a vision for what I call a modern HR.

Consider the power that HR has. It has the power to replicate or disrupt cycles of bias in a company. Recruiting, hiring, promotions, reviews, succession planning, and reporting are all key processes to reconsider in creating a more inclusive culture. HR can either perpetuate systemic roadblocks to marginalized people or become part of the solution.

I'm hardly the first business leader to call for a reimagining and rethinking of HR so that it takes on a key role in both eliminating systemic racism and leading DEI initiatives. We're hearing from HR executives themselves, too, who are recognizing the important role they can play in helping their companies grapple with social-justice issues. "I think the workplace may be the last best place for us to tackle these issues," Steve Pemberton, the chief human resources officer at software firm Workhuman, told *Human Resource Executive* magazine. "You think about your week—where in the course of a week in this voluntarily segregated world are you likely to encounter people of different faiths, ethnicities, languages, generations—all oriented toward a common goal? It's the workplace. I think there's this awareness now that the places where we work can also be the places where we begin to heal."[12]

The fact that there are HR leaders who feel this way should be encouraging, but their hands are tied until the CEO calls them into a meeting and states things explicitly: *We are going to make sure we have the most diverse and inclusive corporate culture possible. I am going to give your teams the tools to be the catalysts for transformation, making it possible for you to build more inclusive systems, to un-bias our existing systems, and to dismantle all structural barriers to inclusion.*

A good example of what modern HR should be: Ragini Holloway, the senior vice president of people at Affirm, has been adamantly steering this financial-technology company—which PayPal cofounder Max Levchin launched in 2012—toward being a leader in DEI in Silicon Valley. That makes Affirm a standout in a place and an industry where for the most part women and people of color are still struggling for inclusion. Because Holloway joined the company in its startup phase, she was able to build a diverse HR group from the ground up, testing a theory that, as she puts it: "If the team that builds out other teams is itself diverse, a grassroots effect will innately permeate companywide hiring practices."[13]

This is key to a culture of diversity. As a CEO, I always built diverse teams and set clear expectations that they, too, would build diverse teams by design.

HR typically has gender diversity but might lack people color. A diverse HR team should be a goal for all companies, even if that goal takes several years to achieve. As an immediate move, however, the head of HR should have a seat on the senior management team and a role in carrying out the vision for a more inclusive workplace.

Holloway points out the need to make sure no one loses sight of the big picture. "It's been important to encourage and often remind my team why hiring for more diversity on our team has been and continues to be critical," she says.

> We've implemented a set of best practices to ensure diversity is top-of-mind in all talent team conversations. These include discussing and reporting on diversity at our regular talent team meetings; prioritizing D&I in all big talent-related discussions; and fostering a team that proactively leads and is involved in the diversity culture at Affirm. We celebrate each time we surpass a goal, but also use the moment to brainstorm new ways to improve in areas where we might be behind on our targets.[14]

Holloway also uses data, which is a crucial component of unbiasing HR. The company's weekly reporting tracks how the company is engaging potential candidates who identify within underrepresented groups (URGs) throughout the recruiting funnel. Says Holloway,

> We do not use these metrics as quotas, and we are intentional about ensuring that we provide equal opportunity and don't overlook qualified candidates from URGs who match our criteria and would add value to our team. Furthermore, our D&I Program Lead spotlights learnings in our weekly talent meetings to ensure that we are constantly discussing new ways of eliminating bias in the interview process, and how we can continue to foster inclusion and a sense of belonging on our team in partnership with our 13 employee resource groups.[15]

You might say that it's a way of helping every HR professional in your organization tap into their own full potential to lead this initiative as they learn to recognize greater potential in others. Then your HR catalysts will understand why continuous self-assessment is critical to their own transformation; biases, whether conscious or unconscious, will stand in the way of a forward-thinking company.

Of course, it's harder to evaluate talent with the levels of specificity I've been talking about than it is to just look for people who fit all preconceived notions of who will be best at the job—though the payoffs are limitless when you turn your organization into a real meritocracy where everyone has a chance to show their potential and keep expanding it. My way requires spending a lot of time getting to know each candidate for a job or promotion. It also requires a new set of communication skills. The language of DEI starts with the way the CEO talks about the company's goal of empowering people, but the HR partners in this effort will be the ones who put it into practice.

It starts, quite literally, with the language that appears when HR representatives post job listings and the language that AI programs use to screen résumés. Large companies routinely use AI to sift through résumés looking for qualifying words so that human HR representatives can start with a preculled stack. AI has many ways of weeding people out, but in an intentionally inclusive culture, the HR department should turn to the many AI tools that help remove bias from hiring as well as from job listings. There is software that deletes identifying characteristics such as name and address, which can be a source of bias in hiring. Further, AI-based gender-decoder tools are designed to go through job descriptions to flag any wording that suggests a male or female bias—or a bias against those of nonbinary gender.[16]

I also believe in retraining HR managers, and everyone else who meets with job candidates, in interviewing skills. If you were to say, "Tell me what you might add to our culture," that opens up a very different perspective from interviewing a candidate to see if she's a culture fit. When I interview people for a position, I expect the conversation to go on for as long as it takes to find out who they really are. I listen more than I talk. I venture prompts like "tell me your story," because it's always interesting to see where people start. I want to know not just what they've done careerwise but also where they come from and what sort of journey they've made. I want to learn how they perceive other human beings, and how inclusive they are in the world. I ask questions about lessons they've learned in their career so that I can get a sense of their capacity for learning and change; ongoing learners are going to be more open to more-dynamic, more-diverse environments. I try to get them to describe what they're passionate about, and where they've found the most success in their careers or in school. That's how I get a sense of what will ignite them in their work.

I've always tried to institutionalize some of this as part of the HR process. The HR interviewer can pair a set of standardized questions with more unstructured, open-ended questions. This allows for a consistency that helps eliminate personal biases while creating space for the humanity of each candidate to come through.

It stands to reason that your HR partners should also be encouraged and incentivized to generate their own ideas for delivering the message about diversity and inclusion. They can be the ones who launch new employee resource groups, initiate and administer community projects, bring in speakers to talk about injustice in society, or run discussion groups to encourage the kind of conversations about race that Howard Schultz envisioned for Starbucks a few years before most of the world was ready for it. More companies are now designing safe spaces where employees can share their experiences; these can be live gatherings or discussions on Slack channels. Either way, a facilitator from HR can be invaluable in encouraging honest feedback about what the organization is doing—or isn't doing—and in providing assurance that senior management will hear about the comments strictly as a way of measuring how well the transformation is going.

As powerful as DEI can be when it's used as an engine for growth and innovation, however, and as beneficial as it can be to everyone when you treat it as a twenty-first-century business strategy, you have to be prepared to encounter resistance. Some people will fear change. When they hear the message that a transformation is underway, it might trigger fears of the unknown, fears of some kind of loss, or fears based on perceptions of their own limitations. When I started at Jamba and announced my agenda, there were several people who left in the first sixty days. It was clear that they were not aligned with the new vision and culture. My style as a leader is to make engagement and participation the norm, so no one can stay disengaged for long. Typically people self-select in or out.

But it's your job as the leader to make sure everyone who *does* stay remains eager to participate and has a voice. It is important to find ways to deliver small wins, to show everyone in the organization that it can be done. The beauty of assigning a business challenge to an action-learning team is that this is an immediate way to prove that new voices will come up with new ideas and innovations. The momentum that results will build on itself. As you begin engaging broader portions of the company, you'll start to see people who might have been left out in the old days contributing more, and that sort of human-capital development speaks for itself.

Key Takeaway

Integrate diversity and inclusion into all of your strategies, values, and incentive systems.

Checklist for CEOs

✓ Design a structure for action learning in which diverse teams are assigned to come up with new business ideas.

✓ Develop your personal strategy and style for discussing race, racism, and diversity, including the terminology you're going to use.

✓ Provide workshops in constructive dialogue and require all managers and employees to attend them.

✓ Examine the messages the company communicates through its content and physical spaces, and make sure they reflect a culture of diversity and inclusion.

✓ Handpick a core group of executives, HR managers, and middle-level managers to be catalysts for change.

✓ Meet with the core group to discuss their role in leading a more inclusive culture.

✓ Design a modern HR system with a key role in eliminating racism and leading DEI initiatives.

5

Building Inclusive Leadership into the Company DNA

F or at least half a decade before the Black Lives Matter movement came to the fore in the corporate sector, the smartest business leaders were talking about the importance of inclusive leadership—a concept I've defined here:

> **Inclusive leadership** builds inclusive work environments, values diversity, and inspires individuals and teams to unlock their full potential by bringing their full selves, unique experiences, and perspectives to the organization.

Michael C. Bush, the CEO of the workplace-culture consulting firm Great Place to Work, has described a new breed of business executives who "transcend traditional leadership approaches that don't keep up with today's economic and political challenges. They embody emerging mindsets and skills like humility, empathy, and learning agility. They are the drivers of innovation and are setting the pace for the future of work." Bush calls these executives for-all leaders.[1] His description is right in line with the bold strategic vision that I talked about in the last chapter, the vision that has to come from the CEO and senior managers because only the leaders have the power to carry out big strategic changes in an organization. Once you've adopted the vision of an inclusive, for-all leader, however, the design you've created for a transformation must now be integrated into the workplace and embedded in the culture, values, performance, and incentive systems.

How do you instill inclusive leadership at every level? In my consulting practice, Culture Design Lab, when I talk to CEOs and other executives who want to bring about change, I ask them to draw a diagram of the organizational chart. This is a literal drawing, but I also ask them to describe the layers of management and how many people report directly to the senior-level managers, then the next level, and then the next. By diagramming your organization this way, you will find the key you need to unlock cultural transformation. (See figure 5-1.)

You look at these layers one by one because you're seeking the answer to a crucial question: Who are the managers who have the largest number of employees reporting directly to them? In every organization, you'll find that critical change lever somewhere in middle management. They're the people most responsible for carrying out any new processes. They are also responsible for setting the career paths of others. At a supermarket chain, most of the workforce might report to district managers. At a restaurant chain, it's usually

FIGURE 5-1

For-all leadership model: middle managers as catalysts for change

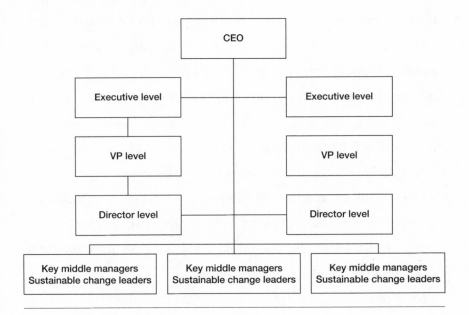

the district or regional operating leaders who run a certain area. At a consumer-goods company, it will probably be the cross-functional leaders at a director level in sales, marketing, manufacturing, and technology. At a restaurant operation with several thousand locations and 100,000 employees you might have 150 middle managers. They are the people who are most responsible for the careers of the staff, so their actions and decisions have a powerful impact.

The key to driving sustainable change lies in reaching down the chain of command to the middle managers and giving them the tools and incentives to carry out the changes, because their domain is where most of the people in the organization reside.

In chapter 4, I talked about enlisting middle managers as your hand-picked catalysts for change. You don't have to bring in every middle manager from every division of the company, although that is certainly desirable in some businesses, but you should pick managers from the most critical business lines to be part of the initial team of catalysts. There are many ways to form such a team. Eventually you will expect all managers and supervisors to be change leaders, but you can roll out inclusive-leadership initiatives in phases. I advised a national chain that introduced its cultural changes in several stages by geographic region. On the other hand, if you have, say, ten facilities, each with a manager who falls into the category of critical middle management, you might start with bringing two or three of those managers into your team of catalysts and have them inform change throughout the workforce.

We often hear about middle management as the "frozen" layer where new initiatives and strategies go to die. When that happens, it's largely because the company's senior leadership has failed to give those middle managers the education and the tools they need to lead change. An important cross-industry study by Behnam Tabrizi of Stanford University revealed that in a randomly selected group of companies, the majority of large-scale change and innovation efforts failed. However, a hallmark of the 32 percent of companies that were successful in making transformative changes was "the involvement of mid-level managers two or more levels below the CEO. In those cases, executives weren't merely managing incremental change; they were leading it by working levers of power up, across and down in their organizations."[2]

Middle managers have a tough job. Lisa Wardell, former CEO of Adtalem, kept an eye on the challenges her middle managers faced when it came to carrying out DEI policies, and she says that without strong guidance and support from above, those managers were perpetually caught between the demands from senior management and the need to ensure daily performance.

"The underlying reason a diversity initiative doesn't get past middle management is not intent," she says. "It's about fear of doing something or saying something wrong. That is why people don't take risks. It's why there aren't talent moves that challenge the status quo. As a middle manager, you might have a team of three people and they all happen to be white males. That's your team—so you'll wonder if you're being asked to switch out someone unless the senior leaders let you know that it's a journey. Then, once you get someone in there who may not think the same way as you do, you have to have a forgiving environment to make things work."[3]

At the same time, it's imperative that your middle managers have decision-making powers. That's a function of the times we live in. John Chambers, the former CEO of Cisco, addressed a conference hosted by Great Place to Work in 2017, in which he talked about the accelerating speed of change and the demands that that will place on the workplace of the future. "Companies won't be able to win if they wait for senior executives to learn about problems and make decisions," said Chambers. "You're going to have information coming into your company in ways you never imagined before. Decisions will be made much further down in the organization at a fast pace."[4]

It's up to you as a senior leader to make sure your middle managers can succeed as great leaders for the twenty-first century. That means they'll need to be invested with the authority to make decisive assignments, hires, promotions, and policy changes within their area, and they'll need to know they have the ear of senior management when it comes to reporting ideas, problems, and new developments. If they don't have a full set of tools to operationalize diversity and inclusion, the initiative is doomed, no matter how eagerly the senior teams promote it.

Let's look at how you build and scale inclusive leadership purposefully and patiently by engaging middle management. My strategy for getting these key catalysts on board can be divided into two main components that are broad but full of complexities, and designed for the long haul:

1. Lay out all of your expectations.

2. Embark on a multiyear journey of change.

Lay Out All of Your Expectations

Make it crystal clear: you expect every leader to intentionally build a diverse workforce with inclusive work environments. At the heart of everything, you are training this group of catalysts to be the business leaders of the future. Start the conversation by discussing *why* you're asking them to change the way they've been leading people. It's because great companies—those that are the most profitable over the long term, those that show the most consistent value over time—know that everyone in the organization counts. Great companies understand that business success depends on developing all of the talent at every level of the organization.

The middle managers you choose as change catalysts may have heard the business case for diversity and inclusion before, but they might not be fully aware of how a DEI strategy can become a part of the overall business strategy. You can talk about why diversity and inclusion will lead to growth through greater innovation, and how you plan to deploy the strategies discussed in chapter 4 to get there.

Present data showing the numbers. The analysis you've conducted that shows the racial and gender composition of your company's work-force can also be broken down by divisions within the organization, so that each middle manager knows how his or her division compares with others in the organization and among industry competitors. Set goals for hiring and promotions; for example, the number of new hires or promotions that should be Black, Latinx, Asian, female, or LGBTQIA+ in each division. Set target dates for these goals, and make it clear that for the middle managers, performance evaluation and compensation (more on that later in this chapter) will be closely tied to attracting and keeping a diverse workforce.

At the same time, let your middle managers know that senior management has their backs and is going to remove barriers and give them the tools they need to meet those goals. Everyone will need time—possibly a year or two—to deconstruct the way they've approached hiring, assignments, and promotions. Diversity is always kind of messy up front, because you have to process how an infinite variety of people see the world.

A 2020 study from Catalyst, the global organization that provides thought leadership on creating more inclusive workplaces for women, contains some valuable lessons to impart to your middle management change agents, starting with "get comfortable with the uncomfortable." Here is more advice from Catalyst:

- Focus on learning, being humble enough to say, "This is more difficult than I want it to be or expected," and courageously commit to doing things differently.

- Let go of your desire to be right. Consider that the way others may solve a problem or take initiative could be just as effective as your way of doing things, if not more so.

- Focus on helping your employees take ownership of their work. Give them the tools and support to execute on goals and to take great pride in their accomplishments and sense of collaboration.

- Speak up when you see biased behavior. Silence is not support. Allyship is about intentional action that demonstrates support for individuals or groups who are marginalized or underrepresented.[5]

Present an initiative for promoting those who are underrepresented at the top

What is equally important to keeping your middle management catalysts engaged instead of resistant is positive reinforcement from the top. If, for example, there are initiatives underway to promote underrepresented people to the top, that sends a powerful message to everyone in the organization—and it will help middle managers attract and retain diverse hires. A brilliant example of this is the plus-one approach that Chief Diversity Officer Erby Foster put into action at Clorox.

The idea was that the company could build in change simply by adding diverse leadership incrementally but with an effort to add those diverse leaders across all departments and functions. Within each division, the company should proactively identify knowledge or experience gaps on senior teams and bring in people from diverse backgrounds to fill the gaps. As Foster points out, if you have an ethnically diverse senior team but they all went to the same business school, that isn't true diversity, because they've all learned to approach business problems the same way, so you'll still have some blind spots that forestall innovative thinking. In that case, it's important to look further afield, another degree. Hence, plus one.

To identify such gaps, the senior executive teams at Clorox conducted an executive inventory. In less than a year, nearly thirty teams evaluated their makeup and added new people who could bring diversity of thought. Clearly, this kind of intentional diversity creates immediate changes it the composition of a company's leadership. It's an excellent way to make sure that you spotlight very capable people of color and make them part of a structure that will remove or dismantle impediments to progress. It also has a strong impact further down the organization.

"If a Black person gets promoted to a senior position, all of the Black employees have a sense that 'we got promoted,'" says Foster. "They see that the company is making some progress, so they want to stay."

I've been in that situation myself. At Nestlé Purina I was promoted thirteen times in fifteen years, and as I moved up the ladder, I founded and led employee resource groups and promoted others who had previously been overlooked. White executives often don't realize that when you have the first person of color step into a top position, it tells others that they, too, can achieve their dreams. We saw that when Barack Obama became the first Black president, and more recently, when Kamala Harris became the first African American and the first woman to hold the office of vice president. Roxanne Jones, a founding editor of *ESPN The Magazine* and former vice president at ESPN, wrote eloquently of the impact: "Harris' journey inspires Black women and girls to break out of the boxes that dictate how we fill up space in the world. It shows us how to pivot and walk freely as multidimensional, unapologetic Black women. We don't need to be chameleons, changing constantly to fit in."[6]

The doors are beginning to fly open. People of color and other minority groups will start finding opportunities elsewhere if their present employer makes them feel marginalized. Employers that lose potential talent this way will be hard-pressed to catch up with more inclusive competitors.

Show your managers how to interrupt bias

I don't believe that you can eliminate systemic racism and biases just by throwing money at antibias training, but it is very important to help everyone in the organization recognize how biases might affect their actions. When you let your middle managers know that inclusive leadership is going to be mandatory from here on, and biases will not be tolerated, you will most likely have to show them the way to a more inclusive management style.

This is no small feat. Biases are deeply ingrained and often unconscious. You'll have to change mindsets and change the ways individuals communicate with one another and the judgments they make in the course of a day. Yet it's a transformation that you instill through concrete steps and programs. The first step is your own intentional efforts to weed out bias. At all times, show your teams what you expect by leading through example.

I've talked already about how Lisa Wardell makes a point of calling people out on biased behavior when she feels it's necessary—thereby letting everyone in the room see inclusive leadership in action. In another example, she tells a story of a meeting with two men and a woman from a company that had a service to sell. All three were white, but in this case the bias was directed at the woman, a young junior executive who was also the one who had done the research and given the presentation.

"I was asking questions, and the woman—I'll call her Meghan—was answering them," says Wardell. "The men were letting her speak, yet every time she closed her mouth, one of the men would jump in with 'What Meghan is saying is . . ." or 'just to reiterate . . .' as if a woman wasn't capable of making things clear. I finally told them, 'If I don't understand what Meghan is saying, I will let you know. Until then, I'm good.'"[7]

The way Wardell spoke out is one example of being a "bias interrupter." This is a term that comes from my colleague Joan Williams, a law professor and founding director of the Center for WorkLife Law at the University of California Hastings College of the Law. Williams has documented how subtle forms of racial and gender bias are transmitted through organizational cultures and systems. To call out the deeply rooted expectations that influence our views of people and their abilities, she has created a series of tool kits called bias interrupters, which she defines this way: "Bias interrupters are tweaks to basic business systems (hiring, performance evaluations, assignments, promotions, and compensation) that interrupt implicit bias in the workplace, often without ever talking about bias."[8]

Besides injecting bias interrupters into the conversation when needed, a CEO should institutionalize them as part of operational practices and policies. I have used bias interrupters in many ways. Requiring that a diverse slate of candidates be considered for any open role is a form of bias interruption. So is having white managers attend Black and Latinx MBA conferences and using action-learning teams to integrate diverse voices into key projects and expose nondiverse leaders to wider talent in the organization.

But there's more you can do. Let your middle managers and other key catalysts know that they too will be expected to act as bias interrupters. Addressing structural racism requires having managers who understand the specific ways bias commonly privileges one group, so that they can understand the reasoning behind the new policies, procedures, and incentives. Accomplishing this will require antibias training, but it must be training that does more than just explore the cognitive bases of bias; it must provide concrete strategies for interrupting it.[9] Williams's "Individual Bias Interrupters" workshop does this by explaining how bias plays out on the ground and by giving managers time to brainstorm ways they personally would feel comfortable interrupting it. Facebook is doing something similar in its inclusion training sessions, which give people a chance to brainstorm ways to interrupt bias. Make this kind of training part of the structure: all training, from onboarding to leadership programming, should seamlessly build in continuing education on how bias enters into company culture, at many evidence-based, meet-you-where-you're-at touch points.

There will be many such opportunities to interrupt biases as you begin the journey to inclusive leadership.

Embark on a Multiyear Journey of Change

We know that it's going to take several years to reach your goals, so all of your managers and catalysts for change will need to know that you have patience. Present the action plan, asking middle managers to start with easy wins that they can achieve in the first quarter, such as a community-engagement initiative, recruiting interns from historically Black colleges and universities, or launching a supplier-diversity program. Such steps will help build momentum.

Use the momentum to gain more buy-in for a more diverse approach to hiring and assignments. What I've always taught my HR group about interviewing job candidates applies to all organization leaders when they're evaluating candidates for a new job or an important assignment. Have a long conversation with every interested candidate. Don't set time limits; let the conversation go on as long as it takes to find out who this person really is. Ask candidates questions that will encourage them to talk about what they can bring to the organization beyond their work experience.

Talk with your middle managers, too, about who they have selected for top assignments in the past year and why they've selected those people. No doubt perceived potential plays an important role in their selections, but what led them to see that potential? Was it just a matter of someone showing enthusiasm, having impressive educational credentials, or previous experience? Was it a perception of "leadership" qualities or of someone being a "a good fit"?

Middle managers have many balls to juggle when it comes to evaluating their staff, solving problems, and keeping both productivity and team morale high—all of which are important components of a sustainable culture of inclusion. Three of the most useful tools you can provide to help them meet these demands are giving them instrumental roles in action-learning teams, guiding them in their assignment decisions, and training them to spot and interrupt bias.

Make middle managers a part of every action-learning team

I always recommend that middle managers be represented on every action-learning team because they bring an important functional perspective of what can be accomplished. In particular, handpick several middle managers to serve on action-learning teams that are looking at how to achieve greater diversity and inclusion throughout the company, so that those managers will be at the forefront of the transition and see for themselves how previously unheard voices can emerge as leaders when they have the opportunity.

In addition, middle managers are typically the people who decide who is going to get the career-enhancing assignments and future promotions—a task that includes making assignments to action-learning teams. For those who participate in action-learning teams, the work they do becomes a stepping-stone to promotions or to top rankings when it comes to performance reviews, generating new business, sales numbers, and such—which is one of the reasons it's so important to have a diverse slate of participants. The middle managers you enlist as catalysts for change will have the important task of scoping out potential and choosing who else serves on these teams.

Keep everyone on the alert for biases

As I've noted, all of the organization's leaders are going to be engaged in an ongoing effort to eliminate bias—their own and that of others, conscious and unconscious. By continuously identifying and interrupting biases, you begin to incorporate a new communication style into the organization. The very language that managers use in hiring, performance reviews, assignments, promotions, and compensation will have to evolve to reflect more inclusive practices. The message to be inclusive comes first, but as you start requiring managers at every level to reflect on how they're judging people and why, they will have to pay closer attention to each individual's specific contributions and potential. Middle managers, because they interact closely with a large number of employees day to day, have a particularly influential role to play here in being on the alert for biases at every touchpoint.

They will also need to be aware of their own biases, and part of their training must guide them in recognizing how they judge people. For example, bias interruption is critical when it comes to the way your managers review their staff. Make meaningful performance reviews an integral part of the system. To be meaningful, employee evaluations must be specific. I've always required my managers to state examples so that it's clear they aren't just making assumptions, which can be reflections of blind spots. Otherwise, you risk a culture in which managers and colleagues might reflexively label a Black woman "aggressive" or an Asian employee "reserved" without actually analyzing what that individual has done to earn those adjectives. This is exactly the kind of culture that says "he has a lot of potential" when evaluating a young white male, while young Black employees have to prove what they can do.

Joan Williams says a performance review should begin with criteria directly related to the job requirements, so that you present evidence of a person's capabilities. For example: "He is able to write an effective summary judgment motion under strict deadlines," instead of, "He writes well." Rather than saying simply, "She's quick on her feet," you might say, "In March, she gave X presentation in front of Y client on Z project, answered his questions effectively, and was successful in making the sale." This way, the manager has to keep observing and documenting how effectively her staff members are doing their jobs—so that every evaluation of performance or potential comes with proof.

Keep track of DEI metrics

When a company's leaders are trying to solve a problem, they gather evidence, set goals, and compile a set of metrics they can use to analyze their progress. As we often say in the business world, if it matters, measure it—so the fact that metrics have long been absent from DEI agendas speaks volumes. In chapter 3 I talked about auditing the culture and setting benchmarks for your progress. As you're building an inclusive culture, collecting data will continue to be key.

Data analysis will help you identify where the biases are and let you continually gauge how antibias measures are working. Culture is defined by *what* we measure. Does your company measure the racial, ethnic, gender, and LGBTQIA+ composition in such areas as talent acquisition and development, talent retention, and supplier diversity? You won't know what you have until you start keeping score.

The data should provide a complete evaluation of how the company finds job candidates, what questions are asked and what is measured in the interview process, how performance is assessed, how promotions are structured, and how the company handles complaints, reprimands, and dismissals. The exact metrics will vary from one organization to another, but the goal is always to measure the frequency of practices that indicate bias.

Take, for example, a measurement of how many people consistently receive top performance ratings and who those people are. Do your performance evaluations show consistently higher ratings for straight white men than for people of color, women, LGBTQIA+ employees, or other groups? Do employees' ratings fall after they take parental leave or become involved in efforts to increase diversity? I'm thinking, in the lattermost case, of the criticism of Google's treatment of minority employees, sparked when Timnit Gebru, a Black woman whom the *New York Times* called "a respected artificial intelligence researcher," was fired from the company, a firing allegedly tied to her criticism of minority hiring and biases built into Google's AI systems.[10] Data should capture all of the patterns in the way people are evaluated.

Similarly, metrics should be used to give you a snapshot of who is being hired and promoted, whether people are truly receiving equal pay for equal work, who feels they are getting all of the tools they need to excel at their job—and even who feels their contributions to the organization are valued and who is happy with their job. Are the results skewing in ways that show an underappreciation of underrepresented groups? If so, then you know what needs to change.

At Jamba Juice, we polled employees on these questions every quarter. Bonuses for middle managers—in our case, that was general managers for each Jamba Juice café and district managers for the cafés under their jurisdiction—depended in part on the overall health of the culture and on employee engagement as measured in the survey. The other part of their compensation was determined by customer experience, which we measured in a separate survey that customers were asked to fill out online or by phone in return for a discount on their next purchase.

You can also use analysis to evaluate the evaluators. Williams suggests appointing people in the organization to be bias interrupters for multiple purposes—a role that either the chief diversity officer or a group of key catalysts from the HR team might play—and one of their key mandates should be to provide what Williams calls "bounceback." That is, they make a point of identifying managers and supervisors whose performance assessments consistently show lower ratings for certain groups of people, and then talking through the evidence with them. For example, says Williams in the bias interrupter training materials on her website, "when a supervisor's ratings of an underrepresented group deviate dramatically from the mean, the evaluations are returned to the supervisor with the message: either you have an undiagnosed performance problem that requires a performance improvement plan or you need to take another look at your evaluations as a group."

Middle managers should be kept informed on all of this data so that they know how they stack up. They should be able to compare data from their own division with that of others, as well as with that of the company in general. They should be told if their departments consistently show lower performance ratings for certain groups of people. That way they will know when they themselves have work to do, while those who have a great track record for inclusive management can work with other managers who need improvement, perhaps through brainstorming sessions and action learning.

All along the way, of course, they will need senior management to support the recruiting and development of diverse talent, and to make it clear that diversity is mandatory and will be monitored. During his tenure as CDO at Clorox, Erby Foster developed a training intensive that gave the company a ready pipeline of women and minorities with the credentials to begin advancing their careers. From there, he tracked the promotions that occurred and held division managers accountable for promoting a certain number of underrepresented people from within the company each year. Managers received bonuses for meeting minority-representation goals. Even so, when one manager said he just didn't know of enough qualified minorities and was willing to sacrifice his bonus, it became clear why the CEO must be the one who guides diversity mandates. In a case like that, the CEO has to step in and show the manager that his low diversity numbers are dragging the whole company down. Ultimately the resistant manager at Clorox saw how much of an impact he could make.

"So," says Foster, "I asked him to become the executive sponsor for the Black employee resource group so that he could help influence their role in the company." That was another tactic Foster used regularly: at some point, nearly every senior executive acted as a sponsor for an ERG. As a result, the senior executives developed a personal interest in the careers of underrepresented individuals and became advocates for them. Those personal connections, he says, helped eliminate a lot of bias.[11]

Link managers' compensation to their DEI metrics

About those bonuses for good diversity numbers. It's great to be able to tell all of your executive and management teams that they're receiving a priceless opportunity to grow as powerful leaders for the future, but money speaks even louder.

People don't like change and, at least subconsciously, know they can stop change just by ignoring it. That is particularly true of middle managers, because of their key role in the trajectory of so many careers. But at every level, you have to give people reasons to embrace the change. Part of that is a no-brainer principle: if you affect their compensation, you have their attention.

The incentive structure for helping create an inclusive culture needs to be tied directly to the goals you've established. At Jamba Juice, we instituted a new incentive system in which up to 20 percent of store managers' compensation was determined by the engagement, climate, and organizational-health scores that came from continually measuring our progress through a variant of the Gallup Q^{12} survey.

I've been consulting with a company that measures its year-end manager assessment based on how well the manager has done when it comes to building a future talent pipeline, building a leadership team, and achieving the company's numerical goals for diversity.

Medallia CEO Leslie Stretch has instituted an incentive system in which 100 percent of his leadership teams' equity compensation is based on increasing Black representation so that it is on track to reach at least 13 percent by 2023—matching Black representation in the US census. McDonald's is tying 15 percent of executives' bonuses to meeting DEI targets, with an aim to have 35 percent of its US senior management come from underrepresented groups by 2025, up from 29 percent when the initiative began in 2021, and increasing the number of women in senior roles worldwide to 45 percent by 2025 and 50 percent by 2030, up from 37 percent in 2021. I should stress that even though the CEO must delegate operational changes, there are no shortcuts. It still begins with having a great leader at the top, and once you've made it clear what you expect from both senior and middle managers, it's more important than ever that as CEO you lead by example. It still falls to the CEO to show that we are all in this together and continually investing in upskilling the workforce so that they will feel relevant and confident.

Empathy must never waver. One of my favorite quotations that I think all leaders should take to heart is from Theodore Roosevelt: "People don't care how much you know until they know how much you care." All that most people in the business world need is a fair chance to be seen for their full selves and talents and passions—and if you give them that kind of chance, they will overdeliver.

Key Takeaway

Middle managers must be key catalysts in creating sustainable change that drives business performance.

Checklist for CEOs

✓ Identify the managers in your organization who are responsible for most of the workforce.

✓ Designate a key group of middle managers as catalysts for change.

✓ Train managers at every level in bias interruption.

✓ Adapt overall company goals to middle management's responsibilities: for instance, hiring and retaining people from underrepresented groups, assigning participation in action-learning teams, learning how to stop bias.

✓ Identify knowledge or experience gaps on senior management teams and promote people from underrepresented groups who can provide what is needed.

✓ Continue to collect data to identify practices that might reflect bias.

✓ Create a compensation structure that is tied to meeting DEI goals.

6

Building an Inclusive Ecosystem

When I joined Jamba Juice, at the end of 2008, unemployment was at a ten-year high and climbing, but nowhere was it worse than in the Black and brown communities. At the peak of the Great Recession, in mid-2010, the unemployment rate in the United States was 9 percent for white workers, 13 percent for Latinx, and nearly 17 percent for Black workers. In this earlier crisis I knew that, even though I couldn't single-handedly rid the country of racism and unemployment, as a CEO I had the clout and the platform to create opportunities for underserved youth in the communities we served.

Under President Obama's Summer Jobs initiatives in 2011 and 2012, we hired more than 2,500 low-income young people, and we partnered with the Treasure Island Job Corps culinary-arts program to offer an internship and mentoring program in the culinary arts, which students used as a pathway to career opportunities.

I knew that I was in a position to help inner-city youth keep healthy and fit so that they could live up to their full potential, so we had a number of programs aimed at raising accessibility to healthy eating in minority communities. We invited high school students from all over Oakland, California, to a "Ready, Set, Jamba Jump" event at which nearly three hundred students jumped rope to music and got a Jamba Juice smoothie afterward. Before the students jumped, they attended a forum with the author and motivational speaker Stedman Graham, who inspired them to pursue their dreams, aim high, and become "the architects in their own lives." We also worked with Bay Area PTAs, providing a Jamba PTA School Appreciation swipe card that Jamba customers could use to pay for their purchase, 10 percent of which would go toward school programs focused on health, wellness, and physical activities.

Activities like these usually fall under the banner of "corporate social responsibility" programs—but I saw them as something integral to our work. A corporation is a microcosm of the world around it. Therefore, if the inclusive culture you are building is going to be sustainable over many decades, you have to invest time and money in building an equally inclusive culture in the world just outside your doors. No, one business leader can't change the whole world, but you do have the power to build a stronger, more diverse ecosystem for all of your stakeholders: consumers, communities, suppliers, employees, and investors. A business ecosystem that espouses the same values you've brought to the rest of your business, eliminating bias and racism and ensuring justice and equity for all, will wield a powerful influence.

Part of what you must do to change mindsets and stamp out bias is attack the problems at the source. That's in schools and universities, where bias causes certain students to be left behind; in communities, where environmental hazards, inadequate health care, underfunded schools, violence, drugs, and myriad other detrimental factors keep people from leading fully productive lives. Also key to attacking at the source: establishing an inclusive culture throughout your entire supply chain. You can't build an intentional culture without the support and participation of your vendors, suppliers, producers, subcontractors, and all other participants in your network. Moreover, as you intentionally build an inclusive supply chain by working with companies owned or operated by people of color, women, and members of the LGBTQIA+ community, you help build wealth within underserved populations.

This is why I say that every CEO should be a change leader. You have high visibility and a platform everywhere that you do business, and your efforts to lead change will have an impact throughout your extended enterprise, as well as on industry peers and other business leaders. Your inclusive culture and value systems will not be sustainable unless they're authentic—and that means you must be intentional and deliberate with every element that your company touches. That includes consumers, clients, communities, colleagues, supply chains, and industry associations. It includes all of your rituals, value systems, and communications.

Why an Inclusive Ecosystem Matters

Every year since 2016, *Fortune* magazine has held the *Fortune* CEO initiative, a conference for purpose-driven corporate leaders. At the

2018 conference, Bryan Stevenson, who is a lawyer and a professor at New York University School of Law as well as the founder and executive director of the Equal Justice Initiative, gave a rather prescient talk titled "The Power of Proximity." Two years before the pandemic, Stevenson told the business leaders in attendance that there was a "trauma epidemic" in Black communities, with 50 percent to 60 percent of children starting school with trauma disorders because of the violence and threats surrounding them—and that the business leaders themselves could play a critical role in the solution through more exposure to those communities.

"I believe that to make a difference in creating a healthier community, a healthier society, a healthier nation, and thus a healthier economy, we've got to find ways to get proximity to the poor and the vulnerable," said Stevenson.

> I absolutely believe that when we isolate ourselves, when we allow ourselves to be disconnected from those who are vulnerable and disfavored, we sustain and contribute to these problems. . . . In proximity there is something we can learn about how we change the world, the environment, how we create healthier communities . . . Even if we don't have any answers about what we're going to do when we get there, the power is in proximity. Many of us have been taught if there's a bad part of town, don't put your business there, stay as far away from that segment of the community as possible. We need to do the opposite . . . At a very minimum, we can find collective and institutional and meaningful ways to embrace

these communities, and sometimes it is that witness that can be transformative.[1]

He went on to say that change is going to happen only when we're willing to do things that are uncomfortable and inconvenient. "It only happens when good people place themselves in difficult places, and they become witnesses," he said.

This was a talk designed to hit a nerve among those in highly privileged positions. In the time since, we've been through the national awakening after the murders of George Floyd and Breonna Taylor. We've been through a global pandemic that proved, to anyone who might have harbored any doubts, that those who are Black, brown, poor, or underserved are far more vulnerable than the privileged to catching the disease and suffering the most-devastating effects. We *should* be uncomfortable with these facts. We should also recognize that we're in a position to make changes in society and be role models for the next generation of business leaders.

We've seen the call to change in the Business Roundtable statement that "U.S. corporations play a vital role in American society as engines of creativity, innovation and economic opportunity. The long-term success of these companies and the U.S. economy depends on businesses investing in the economic security of their employees and the communities in which they operate."[2] We've seen numerous studies showing that, especially since 2020, the American public expects business leaders to guide the country toward greater social justice. I've talked about the importance of empathy, but you don't make an impact unless you accompany empathy with action.

Empathy Plus Action Equals Impact

Archbishop Desmond Tutu of South Africa put it even more strongly: "If you are neutral in situations of injustice, you have chosen the side of the oppressor."[3] This is where we are today; society has high expectations of CEOs, and if you are silent, you will appear neutral. And in a world where social-media messages can turn things upside down at the touch of a button, we all have to be proactive. Anything else will look like silence.

Quaker Oats was a company that waited too long to make an important change to its blatantly retro, racist Aunt Jemima brand of pancake syrups and mixes, although Quaker and its parent company, PepsiCo, are now making amends. Social-media pressure against the brand was fierce. In a TikTok video titled "How to Make a Non-Racist Breakfast," which had more than 4.5 million views the last time I looked, a young Black woman named Kirby tells viewers about how the Aunt Jemima character was inspired by minstrel shows, and the original model for the character, Nancy Green, was a former slave. The video concludes with Kirby saying, "Black Lives Matter, people—eat another breakfast," while dumping a box of Aunt Jemima pancake mix down the kitchen sink. In 2020 Quaker Oats finally announced it would change the "Mammy" image on its Aunt Jemima products, and in early 2021 it rebranded entirely; we can now have pancakes and syrup from the Pearl Milling Company, named after the original mill in St. Joseph, Missouri, that began making the pancake mix in 1889.

The change was essential, but it needs to be accompanied by continued action to show that this is part of an authentic cultural transformation. A 2020 case study of the Aunt Jemima brand stresses that the new brand should be a force for good. The study notes that PepsiCo is taking a number of positive actions, with a five-year, $400 million commitment to fund a range of initiatives that include increasing the number of Black managers by 30 percent by 2025, doubling PepsiCo's sourcing from Black-owned companies, and funding scholarships for four hundred Black community-college students.

Of course, Quaker's image overhaul is an extreme example. Few among us make products that hark back to slavery. Still, every CEO should be prepared at all times to make a statement when the moment calls for it. It can be just a matter of taking a courageous stand, as when Nike kept Colin Kaepernick on as a brand ambassador after he'd protested racism and police brutality by kneeling instead of standing during the playing of the national anthem at NFL games. While there were boycotts, Nike saw its stock rise 5 percent in the month after Kaepernick appeared in a television and print ad celebrating the thirtieth anniversary of the Just Do It campaign with the slogan: "Believe in something. Even if it means sacrificing everything. Just Do It."[4]

Better yet, however, is to be at the forefront, anticipating how your products and expertise can be harnessed to contribute to the greater good. Lisa Wardell thought ahead once again when it came to emergency relief programs in the early days of the pandemic. Since Adtalem operates schools for health-care professionals, Wardell started looking at what the company could do to assist those in the front lines and in low-income communities. Through its foundation, Adtalem donated $300,000 to the American Nurses Foundation and to A Better Chicago, an organization dedicated to supporting low-income Chicagoans, all to assist with economic and mental-health support. The company also provided hard-to-procure medical supplies and personal protective equipment—including N95 masks, gowns, gloves, and sanitizer—to health-care systems across the United States and to local relief organizations in the Caribbean. Other programs included assembling an independent student volunteer group to assist frontline workers with services like running errands and providing child and pet care during the pandemic, and a #CareForCaregivers campaign that provided a number of support services for frontline workers. That's just a few of the ways Adtalem continues to take action. Longer-term initiatives include a strategy for reducing the company's environmental impact, with an eye especially toward areas where it operates that are vulnerable, such as the Caribbean, and through both its financial-services division and the Association of Certified Anti-Money Laundering Specialists, an initiative to combat modern-day slavery and human trafficking.

In another example of reaching throughout the ecosystem, Adtalem's Ross University School of Veterinary Medicine is working with environmental agencies on the island nation of St. Kitts with a goal to develop sustainable food production through advanced seafood-cultivation and livestock-breeding techniques.

At Walmart, CEO Doug McMillon made a commitment to spend $100 million to establish a center focused on racial equity following the uprisings for racial justice in the spring of 2020. The aim is to invest funds from the center in programs that will improve racial equity in the areas of criminal justice, education and workforce issues, and financial and health-care systems.[5]

I've said before that the late Bernard Tyson, who was the CEO of Kaiser Permanente, was ahead of his time when it came to creating an inclusive organization, and he was equally proactive in his vision for the world that Kaiser served. In his address to the Great Place to Work for All summit shortly before he died, which in retrospect seems like a stirring summary of his life's work, Tyson talked about the importance of Kaiser Permanente being a partner in the community, taking on issues that disproportionately affect the poor and people of color, such as homelessness, mental health, and food security.

"There are 66 million who live in the communities around us," he said at the summit. "So that's our line of sight. On the homeless issue, it's a combination of the connection of not having a house, or a home, or a shelter, and the impact on health. . . . We believe strongly that if you're going to have a healthy community, you're going to have a healthy family. It starts with having a shelter, a place to go and to call home, and that's our connection of how do we deal with homelessness and affordability. . . . We're working on what we call the shared agenda inside of Kaiser Permanente. It's the shared agenda between Kaiser Permanente and America."[6] Every CEO should consider that: What is your shared agenda with society?

Gain a Competitive Edge through a Diverse Supply Chain

We have heard a lot about the importance of a diverse supply chain in recent years, and how a cultural shift here will provide a more innovative range of approaches to problem-solving and ideas in general. To my mind few CEOs have done more to make supplier diversity a competitive advantage with a continuous economic impact than Brian

Cornell at Target. Between 2016 and 2018, Target increased its business with suppliers owned or run by women or people of color by 64.4 percent. In 2020 the retailer spent almost $1.5 billion with diverse suppliers, and in 2021 announced a commitment to spend more than $2 billion with Black-owned businesses by the end of 2025. Target has pledged to add products from more than five hundred Black-owned businesses.[7]

But why is DEI in the supply chain important? There is a multifaceted business case:

Your partners can help you reach a wider customer base

"Underrepresented businesses are critical to strengthening the great shopping experience we create for our guests," says a statement on Target's website. "By investing in these suppliers, we demonstrate our commitment to building strong partnerships to ensure broader, more innovative assortments, economic development and quality of life for the communities we serve."[8]

When a retail store seeks out diversity in its supply chain, it can also access a more diverse range of products. At Target, that means a chance to broaden its sales by featuring brands personalized for its stores' neighborhoods, and the staff curate special assortments to celebrate cultural moments and milestones.

The retailer's multicultural beauty product lines feature Black- and Latinx-owned brands from rising entrepreneurs, including Black Girl Sunscreen founder Shontay Lundy, The Honeypot's Bea Dixon, and Pacinos' Eric Roa. Asian American owned brands at Target include

Cocokind, a line of organic beauty products that also supports female entrepreneurs; K-Mama's vegan Korean hot sauces; and Sweet Chef, a vegan and cruelty-free skincare line. Target sells products from veteran-owned businesses, including Simplay3 furniture and Maud Borup sweet treats, and from LGBTQIA+-founded brands like Peanut Butter & Co., which makes peanut butter spreads and powders.

Target also celebrates Black History Month and Hispanic Heritage Month with special assortments and marketing campaigns that elevate Black and Latino/Latina businesses like The Lip Bar, The Doux, and Siete Foods.

A diverse supply chain creates a strong economic impact in places where it's most needed

The National Minority Supplier Development Council estimates that minority business enterprises generate more than $400 billion in economic output annually. A number of companies, including CVS Health, Pacific Gas and Electric, and TIAA issue regular supplier diversity reports analyzing how their relationships with diverse suppliers have contributed to the economy in terms of jobs, wages, and taxes.[9] It's another way to track your progress year by year in building a more inclusive ecosystem and, by extension, a more equitable society.

Target's diverse supply chain includes its work with building contractors, IT, and much more. It has a long-standing partnership, for example, with Thomas Harmon from Black-owned Taylor Bros. Construction Co., which has built dozens of Target stores, and Lili Hall from the Latina-owned marketing firm KNOCK, inc. The retailer supports such partners by investing capital, opening access to new markets, sharing expertise, creating networking and business-building opportunities, and engaging in sponsorships and mentoring to help minority-owned businesses grow.

A diverse and ethically managed supply chain helps mitigate reputational risk

The media and the public are watching, and any problem with racism or bias anywhere in your ecosystem will be seen as your responsibility. Activewear manufacturers learned that lesson way back in the 1990s; recall how Nike, Adidas, and other top brands came under fire after reporters and human-rights investigators exposed the sweatshop conditions in their subcontractors' factories in Asia. Amid boycotts and demonstrations, at first the activewear makers claimed they had no control over their subcontractors—a rationalization that didn't wash with the public. "Quite frankly, that was a sort of irresponsible way to approach this," Nike director of compliance Todd McKean admitted in 2001.[10]

These companies now have ethical employment practices in place for their global subcontractors. Nike has become part of a movement of companies that are transparent about their supply. But consider that the sneaker-sweatshop exposés created a precedent for public outrage well before the age of social media—and now, even the simplest error in judgment can become a global disaster. The Twittersphere was on high alert, for example, when Inditex, parent company to the fashion chain Zara, was shown to be operating grueling, eleven-hour shifts at its Myanmar factories; paying as little as $3.50 to $4.74 per day; and firing hundreds of workers in the middle of the pandemic.[11] The sad thing was that the company was simultaneously contributing to better global public health, turning its eleven factories in Spain, its home country, over to the production of personal protective equipment—which made the contrast in Myanmar look like a statement that Asian lives didn't matter.

The best way to head off controversy is to ensure that your company's value system is reflected throughout the supply chain.

A diverse supply chain is resilient

This is another lesson learned the hard way. When the Covid-19 pandemic hit, the United States faced a shortage of critical emergency medical equipment, especially N95 masks, gowns, and gloves, after many years of offshoring the production of such items. We need to do more local sourcing, seeking the suppliers with the best knowledge of regional demographics.

"We need far better mapping of supply chains so we can identify where shortages will have a cascading impact," says John Nanry, a cofounder of and the chief manufacturing officer for Fast Radius, a Chicago-based manufacturing technology company. Nanry asserts that while we need the US government to create a "manufacturing guard" that would be like a National Guard for manufacturing emergencies, businesses shouldn't wait for that to happen. "Inject fresh talent in the industrial workforce," he advises. "The graying of our workforce has exposed inadequate efforts to recruit and train the young people vital to our future."[12] If you make a commitment to buying from minority-owned suppliers with this kind of potential, perhaps providing investment capital and advisory services to help them

Logitech: How to Commit to Supplier Diversity

Bracken Darrell, the CEO of Logitech, laid it out on the company's website: "We lack Black and other minority representation in our supply base." Logitech's supply chain was not diverse enough, but he was determined to change that. He presented five key actions that Logitech was taking—and that others could follow—for growing the number of suppliers owned by underrepresented groups across the globe. Here he is, in his own words:[a]

- We will require all our future US-based purchasing to include at least two qualified Black, women, or other underrepresented suppliers to be part of the candidate pool (when available).

- Due to systemic inequity, if we are unable to find qualified Black, women, and other underrepresented suppliers, we are going to ask our selected suppliers to submit a clear diversity action plan as a qualifying criterion to win our business. In other words, if we don't find underrepresented suppliers, we're going to demand that our existing ones be more diverse.

- We will make it easier for Black, women, and other underrepresented suppliers to work with Logitech by shortening their payment terms and reducing their contractual obligations. Underrepresented suppliers are often small suppliers who can face barriers in working with corporations, which can impede them in competing for the business, never mind winning the business!

- We will partner with like-minded corporations, diversity action groups (such as the National Minority Supplier Development Council), and international advocacy groups (such as WEConnect) to further support Black, women, and underrepresented suppliers in our own network and beyond through loan programs and investment.

- We are committing to create a supplier development program of Black, women, and other underrepresented groups. To start we will select through this program five to ten suppliers each year for whom we will offer advisory services, pilot projects, network access, and capital.

a. Bracken Darrell, "Our Supplier Diversity," Logitech.com, https://www.logitech.com/en-us/social-impact/diversity-inclusion/supplier-diversity.html.

grow, you'll be creating an economic impact while developing your own resilient supply chain.

This is the way you pave the road to the future, leading the way by fueling economic growth in your company's ecosystem and investing in the talent you'll need in a changing world.

How to Build a More Inclusive Supply Chain

It's time to talk about solutions. There are a number of proven measures that your company can take to develop the kind of supply chain that is critical to keeping your business strong. As I've said, diversity is messy and not always the easiest route. You might have to be proactive in finding minority-led suppliers and contractors, as well as in helping them grow to scale. However, in recent years more and more companies than ever have established models that others can emulate. Here are a number of ways a company can create a fully diverse and inclusive supply chain.

Establish networks through partnerships with professional associations

Professional associations representing minority, women, disabled, and LGBTQIA+ entrepreneurs are eager to partner with business leaders to offer more training programs, conferences, and networking opportunities. More and more industry trade associations have launched their own DEI initiatives and are actively seeking the support and sponsorship of corporate partners. If you can't find an existing organization with a program that fits your agenda for creating a more diverse ecosystem, design your own program and enlist the appropriate associations as partners.

Host your own development programs for minority-owned suppliers

Larger companies in particular are actively developing the suppliers they need. UPS is doing this through partnerships with such organizations as the Women's Business Enterprise National Council, the National Minority Supplier Development Council, and the United States Hispanic Chamber of Commerce, running mentoring and training programs, workshops, professional matchmaking, supplier-diversity conferences, and management education to support the growth and success of diverse suppliers. Coca-Cola runs a supplier-development institute in partnership with Georgia State University, providing education for disadvantaged groups on how to start a business.[13]

Target hosts a Supplier Diversity Summit, where indirect vendors can learn more about Target's processes and business initiatives, while at the same time gaining direct access to Target leaders. Target also hosts both Target Accelerators, a quick, intensive training program for entrepreneurs, and vendor fairs aimed specifically at Black- and Latinx-owned businesses.

Become part of an industry organization that seeks to achieve more-diverse ecosystems

Fair Trade USA, an organization of food, retail, and consumer-products companies committed to operating within an equitable ecosystem, is a good example of how companies can combine forces to build a fairer supply chain. The organization provides a Fair Trade certification to companies that ensure sustainable livelihoods and safe and fair working conditions for their suppliers. Athleta, Dole, General Mills, Green Mountain Coffee Roasters, J. Crew, Patagonia, and Target are among the more than 1,300 companies that have Fair Trade Certified product lines. When companies combine forces this way, they're no longer forced to compete by driving down the prices they pay suppliers—in many cases making it impossible for producers in far off countries to earn a living wage. Fair Trade empowers producers and enables businesses to support sustainable livelihoods and practices more transparently.

The organization continuously seeks opportunities to expand its reach through business partnerships and through the expertise, technologies, and resources provided by philanthropic partners. Businesses that commit to operating a supply chain with safe working conditions, sustainable livelihoods, and environmental protections for all can become Fair Trade Certified companies.

Consumer awareness of the Fair Trade Certified seal was about 63 percent as of 2021, nearly double what it was in 2008. Younger customers are even more interested in buying brands that support social responsibility. A Nielsen survey from 2015 found that 73 percent of millennials around the world said they were more likely to buy brands supporting social issues they care about.[14]

Needless to say, when Fair Trade Certified companies work with their suppliers to ensure fair working conditions in their factories and on their farms, they are improving life for people of color in many parts of the world.

The Justice, Equity, Diversity, Inclusion (J.E.D.I.) Collaborative for the natural-products industry is also working with producers and vendors to develop systematic DEI principles within the fair-trade model. The collaborative is talking about how to create a natural-products industry that yields a strong, positive impact wherever it sources ingredients and production; that brings in the voices of marginalized communities; and that reaps the innovations to be found when you have a diversity of identities and perspectives. J.E.D.I. is looking at DEI in a bigger, more global way, instilling the principles of an intentional anti-racist culture throughout the supply chain and the greater ecosystem.

All industries should be looking at building inclusive industry-wide practices for their supply chains; otherwise, they'll miss out on critical perspectives.

It's Time to Take the Lead

To start building an anti-racist, unbiased ecosystem, take these three steps:

1. Consider your role in the community, and how a proactive approach to solving problems would enhance your business.

2. Sponsor programs that are part of your shared agenda with society so that you can have a sustainable impact on the ecosystem around you.

3. Run a risk assessment of your supply chain and seek out partners that will provide resilience and open doors to new markets.

It's hard to look at your ecosystem and not see that you have years and years of work ahead. I'm challenging business leaders to build partnerships and systems from the ground up, in some cases becoming agents of change in a vast global network of suppliers. Yet this is the way to grow your business in the 2020s, tapping into the best minds everywhere and being resilient against a climate of unforeseen risks that, as we're all learning, is becoming a way of life. Moreover, intentional business leaders have already banded together to create a growing number of resources (see the lists in the appendix) so that no one has to take the lead alone—and no one can afford to overlook the changing world that's emerging all around us.

Key Takeaway

Building an anti-racist organization requires reimagined structures that drive diversity, equity, and inclusion throughout every corner of the ecosystem.

Checklist for CEOs

This time, the tasks are philosophical:

- ✓ Get comfortable with being uncomfortable: recognize that you are in a position to improve social justice.

- ✓ If you spot an injustice, be vocal and proactive about changing it.

- ✓ Look for ways that your business can be a force for good in the community.

✓ Seek out minority-owned businesses as suppliers and contractors and invest in their growth.

✓ Quantify and publicize the economic impact coming from your supplier relationships.

✓ Design your own programs to reach diverse suppliers and the communities you serve, in partnership with organizations that can help scale your work.

7

Culture Is the Key That Unlocks the Future, and the Future Is Now

What will the workplace of the future look like?

We are on a march forward, dismantling old racist social structures in the United States and rebuilding them into for-all workplace cultures. At the same time, technology is changing the corporate world as we've known it. The shift to a greater number of virtual offices, accelerated by the pandemic, is giving rise to a powerful case for a workplace that includes the best minds for a multicultural, multisegmented world.

Creating such a workplace will require continued intentional effort, however. It will take years to change the white-dominated corporate culture that was built on a four-hundred-year-old legacy of structural racism, with only gradual adjustments as women and minorities began making professional inroads. In the 1950s, it was not uncommon to see "Help Wanted" sections of daily newspapers with jobs categorized as "White" and "Colored," "Male" and "Female." Seven decades later we're still fighting against unconscious biases about who fits into which roles.

In the future, we'll mark 2020 as the year that the Black Lives Matter movement entered the mainstream, coming just at a time when the United States could no longer sweep racism under the rug. It was becoming too obvious that an out-in-the-open white-supremacist movement had the power of weapons, media visibility, and most frighteningly, the support of some political leaders, whether blatantly or surreptitiously. Then, once the pandemic arrived, it became clear that people of color were the most vulnerable to catching and dying from Covid-19. In addition to rampant inequality when it came to access to good medical care, people of color made up a disproportionate number of frontline and essential workers who were exposed to the virus almost as a matter of course, often working without adequate safety protections. I'm pleased to see more CEOs paying attention to the needs of such workers; for example, the forty-some CEOs and business leaders who have created OneTen, an organization that seeks to hire, upskill, and promote one million Black Americans by 2030.

Post-pandemic, companies will have to consider how their policies and practices concerning their frontline workers, including whether they pay them minimum wage, are going to affect the company's reputation and therefore its bottom line.

I like to think that we'll also pinpoint the moment of hope that we witnessed on January 21, 2021, when twenty-two-year-old Amanda

Gorman stood outside the US Capitol and read "The Hill We Climb," the poem she'd been invited to present at the inauguration of President Joe Biden. From the youngest person ever to deliver a poem at a presidential inauguration, we heard these words of wisdom about where we've been in America and where we must go now:

> Somehow we've weathered and witnessed
> a nation that isn't broken
> but simply unfinished.
> We, the successors of a country and a time
> where a skinny Black girl
> descended from slaves and raised by a single mother
> can dream of becoming president
> only to find herself reciting for one.

And further down:

> We are striving to forge a union with purpose,
> To compose a country committed to all cultures, colors,
>   characters and conditions of man
> And so we lift our gazes not to what stands between us
> but what stands before us.
> We close the divide because we know, to put our future first,
> we must first put our differences aside.[1]

My life's work now involves advising corporate executives on developing the inclusive cultures they'll need to meet the needs of tomorrow. I've been duly impressed with the efforts of the CEOs I've worked with, including Todd Schnuck at Schnuck Markets, Matthew Stevens at the Bay Club, Lisa Wardell, formerly at Adtalem, and Leslie Stretch at Medallia, to name a few—especially in the way they insist, no matter what, on standing tall as leaders against racism. That doesn't mean they just declare their companies anti-racist, but that they make a commitment to making sure that racism doesn't intervene with their hiring, promotions, or business practices—and that their anti-racism carries an impact wherever they do business.

"The beauty of anti-racism is that you don't have to pretend to be free of racism to be anti-racist. Anti-racism is the commitment to fight racism wherever you find it, including in yourself. And it's the only way forward," wrote Ijeoma Oluo, author of *So You Want to Talk about Race*, in a July 14, 2019 tweet. Those are wise words for any organization taking on systemic racism.

At the same time, we have to be on guard against losing momentum. After George Floyd was murdered, 66 percent of the companies in the S&P 500 index made statements about racial justice, according to As You Sow, a California group that promotes environmental and social corporate responsibility.[2] That was a good start, but the numbers show that we still have a long way to go when it comes to achieving true diversity and inclusion. As of the first quarter of 2021, these same S&P 500 companies had exactly six Black CEOs: Arnold Donald at Carnival Corp., Craig Arnold at Eaton Corp., René Jones at M&T Bank Corp., Marvin Ellison at Lowe's, and Rosalind Brewer at Walgreens Boots Alliance, and Thasunda Brown Duckett at TIAA (the latter two being the only Black women).

I keep an eye out for companies that issue statements supporting diversity yet still have few Black or brown executives in positions that genuinely contribute to the growth of the business and a more inclusive culture, or still make it clear that they don't care about their front-line employees, custodial contractors, and others who are largely people of color. *Wired* magazine calls this incomplete DEI effort "diversity theater" in an article about tech giants that didn't fully measure up to their own diversity campaigns.[3] At Pinterest, for example, a company that tweeted in support of Black Lives Matter, two Black women on the public-policy team said the company didn't listen to their recommendations. Team member Aerica Shimizu Banks said she found her job performance being criticized after she spoke out against a company decision to stop paying the company's contract catering and janitorial workers for the full holiday week between Christmas and New Year's Day. What I found most notable about the situation was that she said she felt tokenized, as in "'here's our diversity champion . . . but we don't actually want her to do the work we've hired her to do.'"[4]

Doing your part as an anti-racist leader will help ensure that the United States, a country that has benefitted so much at the expense of the marginalized, becomes a society in which everyone can thrive as a productive citizen, adding to the overall wealth and well-being of our society. The alternative, after all, is a civilization that is in danger of crumbling from the chaos that comes with inequality. I could argue about the business, marketing, or public-relations cases for diversity and inclusion until I'm blue in the face, but paramount to all of these is anti-racism's benefit to society.

Change Is Coming

Though we hear about setbacks, I maintain my optimism. What is most important, and is starting to happen, is that business leaders have realized that they have the power to find solutions to any number of societal conditions that have a disproportionate effect on communities of color. And some have realized it's their responsibility to put this power to work, partly because it's the right thing to do, but also because it's the smart thing to do. Take, for example, how in 2020 *Fortune* magazine highlighted the inequities reflected in climate change in a way that just a few years earlier would have appeared only in the left-wing media: "Climate change has roots in economic models, dating centuries back to colonial conquest, that prioritize near-term exploitation of resources and labor at the expense of long-term social and environmental sustainability."[5]

The very tenor of business is moving toward a greater focus on the big picture, taking the long-term view instead of a short-term approach to profitability. The Business Roundtable recommends that, while quarterly reporting is important for transparency, companies should move away from providing quarterly-earnings-per-share guidance in favor of focusing on creating more long-term value. The longer-term strategy, the Roundtable says, "will ultimately increase living standards, expand economic opportunities for Americans and create more room for social improvement."[6] The corporate world has become vested in this long moment of racial reckoning in the United States—and as we embark on the third decade of the twenty-first century, climbing out of the rubble left by the global pandemic, we have a chance to make the necessary restart.

I'm optimistic about corporate America embracing an inclusive culture because I've seen it work so well in my own experiences with companies at the forefront. The world's smartest corporate leaders understand what we're up against when it comes to eliminating racism, what we need to do, and why we need to do it.

I'm encouraged when I see a next generation of leaders built for this moment occupying C-suites across several industries. The always savvy Rosalind Brewer, the new CEO of Walgreens Boots Alliance, for example, has often talked about how she struggled at the beginning of her career to bring her whole self to work. There was a time, she said in a talk with Stanford MBA students, when she tried to dress and talk like the white male executives around her, but it was painfully stressful. Then one day she had to leave work early and decided she would tell her white colleagues exactly why: she had to take her daughter to have her hair braided so that she could participate in a swim meet. "They asked, 'Why are you braiding her hair?'" Brewer recalled. "I had to explain cornrows to the people I worked with. But the more I was like who I am in my personal life, it actually worked . . . There was no shell to peel off."[7]

Brewer has seen that there's a stark difference in the way some people view a Black female leader, but she's forged ahead courageously. As she relayed in a 2019 interview, several years earlier, when she was the CEO of Sam's Club, she had appeared on CNN and said diversity was good for business—and received death threats on social media for the statement. Ironically—but perhaps not surprisingly to those who understand bias—Brian Cornell from Target appeared on the same program after her slot and said virtually the same thing, with no repercussions. Some people don't take it well when the messenger is a woman of color.[8]

Yet more and more, that same message is hitting home. Diversity *is* good for business, and corporate America is finally embracing more than a decade's worth of findings that confirm the business case for DEI. Business leaders are recognizing that they have an important role to play in building a new social structure that embraces diversity and inclusion—and that just having good intentions isn't enough. Think of how Ibram X. Kendi, the author of *How to Be an Antiracist*, spelled out the need for action in an interview with journalist Ezra Klein: "Racist policies are defined as any policy that leads to racial inequity. And so, for me, racial language in the policy doesn't matter, intent of the policymaker doesn't matter, even the consciousness of the policymaker, that it's going to lead to inequity, doesn't matter. It's all about the fundamental outcome."[9]

In addition, as millennials begin making up a growing proportion of the workforce, and Gen Z begins to come of age, the young generations are demanding more as employees and consumers. They are challenging the norms of corporate America, insisting that companies transform with an eye toward justice, diversity, and sustainability. They are fighting for equal pay, for workers' rights at every level, and for companies to take a raw and honest look at their workplace cultures. Companies must adapt now to remain relevant. These realizations, combined with technologies that were already set to revolutionize the workplace before the pandemic and systemic racism

Anti-Racist Moves That Every Business Leader Should Make Now

1. Examine your corporate culture through a DEI lens.

2. Begin a transformation that is led by the CEO and senior executives.

3. Integrate your DEI plans into your business strategy, with quarterly reviews by the board.

4. Make education and training available for every leader and all associates.

5. Create a culture of inclusion with a focus on the competitive advantage it will give you.

6. Build an ecosystem that will thrive in an inclusive economy, starting with a supply chain of companies that embrace DEI.

7. Anticipate that your customer base will hold your company accountable for instilling anti-racist practices.

commandeered the headlines, are going to lead to a corporate environment that looks a lot more like the society we live in. "It'll be a workplace where people like me, magenta afro and all, can be their full selves," my daughter Krista said to me. I think she's right.

In particular, six top trends are starting to turn the old corporate culture on its head. Below, I look at these trends and what every business leader should do to stay ahead of the game.

Conscious capital is pouring into
anti-racist companies

In late 2020, Tom Lynch, the founder of Mill Road Capital Management, launched the firm's Progressive Governance Fund, which practices socially responsible shareholder activism, and I joined the fund as a managing director. Lynch set up the fund to bring modern governance and active engagement to small and mid-cap publicly traded companies, with a focus on driving diversity in the boardroom. We met when we were both serving on the board of Panera Bread, and for four or five years we talked about setting up a fund that would target companies with management teams we believed in and guide them in building the kind of long-term value that comes with an intentionally diverse culture. In 2020 the time seemed just right.

We are asking target companies to improve the culture and character of their boards by appointing enough women and people of color to make up at least 50 percent of the board positions. Small and mid-cap public companies overall are somewhat less diverse than larger companies in the United States, according to Spencer Stuart's 2021 inaugural S&P MidCap 400 Board Report. The study, which Spencer Stuart plans to conduct annually, found that 34 percent of the largest one hundred S&P MidCap 400 companies had no minority directors, while among the two hundred largest S&P 500 companies, only 3 percent lacked minority directors.[10]

We're proud to be part of a growing movement in which investment firms are pushing to level the playing field when it comes to DEI and anti-racism as criteria for their holdings. Large firms such as

BlackRock, Fidelity, and Vanguard have been increasingly emphasizing environmental, social, and corporate-governance (ESG) principles when assessing a public company's merits, but now we are seeing DEI come to center stage among social-activist investor and stakeholder groups, as well as a new wave of intentional investment in anti-racist business activity.

Goldman Sachs is attacking anti-racism with a plan to invest $10 billion over the next decade in companies that benefit Black women through housing, health care, and other programs that are in a position to help narrow the wealth gap in America. *The Wall Street Journal* reports that investments could include anything from industries that employ many Black women, to companies that reskill home-care workers, to community-development financial institutions and health centers.[11]

I'm also working with Black and brown entrepreneurs who have no shortage of big ideas and disruptive technologies but are nevertheless at a disadvantage when it comes to securing funding. (See the section "Keep an Eye on the Next Generation of Business Leaders" below.) According to findings from the US Chamber of Commerce, Black entrepreneurs are nearly three times more likely than white entrepreneurs to see a negative impact on their business growth and profitability due to lack of access to capital.[12] So I'm pleased to see a growth in capital commitments aimed at changing that equation by providing financing to minority-owned businesses. For example, Ariel Investments, the asset manager founded by value investor John Rogers—and one of just a handful of Black-owned investment firms in the United States—is partnering with JPMorgan Chase in a private-equity fund that is committed to investing in minority-owned businesses, particularly by positioning middle-market companies as "leading suppliers to *Fortune* 500 companies."[13]

What to do: Look for emerging companies run by people of color and women that can be part of your supply chain and invest in their growth.

Business leaders are having the tough conversations we need

Some corporate leaders have suggested a national conversation about the past, along the lines of South Africa's Truth and Reconciliation Commission in the 1990s, when the post-apartheid government held hearings in which victims testified about the multiple human-rights violations that occurred under apartheid and perpetrators had a chance to request amnesty, all conducted for the purpose of acknowledging the country's brutal racist past and moving forward.[14] Essentially, that is what I've been advising CEOs to orchestrate in their own organizations: ongoing, honest dialogue, bringing in speakers on the subject of racism to talk to both management and staff, assembling groups for listen-and-learn sessions at regular intervals.

You might make your dialogue program a model for others, perhaps sponsoring sessions with community groups or industry associations and inviting experts on the subject of racism to tell their stories and lead discussions on how to make the future more inclusive.

What to do: Invite experts on the subject of racism to speak to your organization. Commit yourself and take action in support of anti-racism and human rights to show that your company is on the right side of this moment in history.

Industry peers are working together to institute change

We've seen encouraging mea culpas from industries with a history of discrimination; for example, real estate. "What realtors did was an outrage to our morals and our ideals," said Charlie Oppler, the new president of the National Association of Realtors (NAR), at a virtual fair-housing summit in November 2020.[15] He was referring to the active role that realtors have played in enabling housing discrimination, including the industry-wide opposition to passage of the Fair Housing Act in 1968. While much remains to be done, NAR has begun by implementing a new fair-housing campaign and a partnership with the US Chamber of Commerce's Equality of Opportunity Initiative.

What is particularly encouraging, however, is the trend among trade groups and cross-industry groups to bring business leaders together to create new ways to make their industry fully inclusive.

I've mentioned OneTen, a coalition of about forty CEOs and other business leaders who have committed to combining their resources to upskill, hire, and promote one million Black Americans by 2030. The founders are a group of prominent leaders in the business world: Ken Chenault, chairman and managing director of General Catalyst and former chairman and CEO of American Express; Ken Frazier, chairman and CEO of Merck; Charles Phillips, managing partner of Recognize, chairman of the Black Economic Alliance, and former CEO of Infor; Ginni Rometty, executive chairman and former CEO of IBM; and Kevin Sharer, former chairman and CEO of Amgen and former faculty member at Harvard Business School.

OneTen cofounder Ken Chenault says that in order to achieve its goals, the organization will have to work with companies to change their hiring practices, putting a much greater emphasis on apprenticeships, job training, and development programs. "Roughly 75% of Blacks between 18 and 50 who are in the job market don't have a college degree. . . . And so one of the things that is happening is we're re-spec'ing jobs," he told *Fast Company* magazine in 2021. "You can't just say, 'I'm going to work harder and do the same things,' because you're going to get the same result."[16]

The leaders of the Justice, Equity, Diversity, Inclusion (J.E.D.I.) Collaborative have observed that the natural-products industry has traditionally been a mostly homogenous business, led by white executives and entrepreneurs, without much thought to reaching a diverse consumer base or making its products affordable to a wider base. Food growing and distribution are an important component of this industry, so as we see it, J.E.D.I.'s members are in a unique position to be trailblazers, because food is at the nexus of so many pressing social issues.

Access to healthy food, after all, reduces health problems and helps children perform better in school—and all over the world, communities of color lack access to fresh produce. With a more inclusive approach to sourcing, leaders of the natural-products industry can work with farmers on creating scale for sustainable agriculture. Socioeconomic, geographic, and cultural barriers prevent people with marginalized identities from accessing healthy products, and in particular, food. Because food is central to social factors including health, education, and livelihoods, the food industry has the power to create true social change. We know that healthy and culturally relevant food reduces rates of chronic illness, and has positive outcomes on educational performance, and helps communities thrive. So J.E.D.I. is developing tools not just to bring inclusiveness to the industry, but also to make the collaborative a force for solving problems that affect people of color disproportionately, such as food insecurity, economic inequality, and climate change.

In December 2020, J.E.D.I. held a CEO circle in which ten CEOs discussed DEI road maps and where to go from here, including how we're going to measure a company's progress when it comes to building DEI into the cultural fabric. These CEOs are now making material changes in the way they run their businesses. Though these are smaller companies, they have the potential to influence the whole food and natural-products industry. Some of the J.E.D.I. companies will grow into large companies and become industry leaders. Some will be acquired by larger companies that find them attractive targets precisely because the larger companies understand the value to be gained from a reputation for strong DEI practices.

What to do: Join a group of business leaders working to improve racial equity, or form such a group within your industry.

Companies are using action-learning techniques to solve systemic problems

Julie Washington, who is now the chief marketing, communications, and customer-experience officer at Trinity Health, one of the largest multi-institutional Catholic health-care-delivery systems in the nation, likes to compare DEI to a color palette. "When you expand the diversity of colors in your Crayola box, you are able to create brighter images and more-appealing pictures," she says.[17]

She knows firsthand that it takes diversity in the executive suite to ensure that a business has all cylinders loaded when it comes to serving its clientele and community. Trinity Health is an organization that values diverse lived experiences, so she has the ears of senior management when she needs to get a point across. "We go into meetings saying we expect there to be a point of difference," she says. The CEO, Mike Slubowski, has been up front about his own white privilege and his wish to remedy systemic racism. After the George Floyd killing, Slubowski read Martin Luther King Jr.'s *Letter from a Birmingham Jail* and has told colleagues he realized he was the white moderate Dr. King was talking about. With the CEO's leadership, Washington and her colleagues participate in frequent cross-functional and cross-cultural discussions on the projects at hand—using the techniques of action learning.

When Trinity's health-care facilities were having trouble reaching the people who most needed Covid-19 testing, Washington found herself speaking out of her experience—and being heard. "We weren't able to get to Black and brown communities as fast or in as organized a way as we needed to," she says. "To my mind, that meant more people were dying, and nobody seemed to be helping. I started thinking, how do I become the change I want to see?"

One of the main ways people were being tested was through drive-through testing. "I pointed out that if you don't have a car, it's hard to do that," she says. It seems like such an obvious impediment, but if you have a team of people who all come from white, middle-class backgrounds, it might not occur to them. The company began offering tests through more-accessible channels, such as community and church organizations. When vaccines started becoming available,

Washington wanted to launch an information and education campaign for minority and underserved communities, where she knew that a great many people were vulnerable and undecided about the vaccine. The campaign would require budget approval, so Washington figured she should show her colleagues the pain and stress that people of color were experiencing in the pandemic. Her idea: take advantage of virtual church services to see what people in Black congregations were talking about and get it on record.

"On Sundays, I went to virtual churches in Texas, New York, Georgia, and Florida, trying to get a sense of what our people were feeling and saying," she says. "I'd record it, then tell [those who needed to approve the budget] to listen to minutes nine through fourteen, wherever there was a conversation about what people were going through." She got approval for the new campaign.

Different organizations might have their own terminology for the process of teaming up to work out creative solutions to problems—and if the system is truly ubiquitous you might just call it "meetings." The research and advisory firm Gartner envisions that by 2028 it will be standard practice to work in small, flexible, autonomous teams that Gartner calls "we working." Whatever the name, this is the way to stay relevant now and into the future, with cross-functional teams of people who can work fast and decisively to respond to whatever's needed, bringing their insights from their lived experience—and knowing that their colleagues will be eager to hear new perspectives and learn from them.

What to do: Assemble diverse, cross-functional teams to solve business problems, and lean on the diverse viewpoints therein to point out flaws in old assumptions.

Geographic—and cultural—boundaries are blurring

The virtual workplace that became the norm for so many jobs during the pandemic was just a manifestation of where technology was already taking us. Now that we've seen that many jobs can be done remotely, the workplace has become a hybrid of physical and virtual spaces—and in companies where the business model is all digital, sometimes all virtual. The result is a blurring of physical boundaries. Employees don't have to live nearby. If there are few people gathering physically in an office space, and few watercooler or after-work conversations about local sports teams or about who went to what college, it stands to reason that sameness will become less crucial to "fitting in." People will be more concerned that their colleagues exhibit such qualities as fast thinking, trustworthiness, knowledge, and adaptability.

Danny Guillory is the head of diversity, equity, and inclusion at Dropbox, the file-hosting service, which went virtual-first in October 2020—so he now finds himself in the thick of defining what a virtual-first culture should look like. An important part of the plan is to hire people from different backgrounds and perspectives, building a more diverse workforce. "Now we can recruit from the whole country and other parts of the world," says Guillory. "We're going into new territory, and there's going to be a change-management process, making sure managers are open to talent from all over."[18]

To be sure, the corporate world is going to find a number of challenges as it adapts to new ways of working. Guillory's DEI team is using predictive analytics to seek the best outcomes in retention rates—and finding, not surprisingly, that people from underrepresented minorities are most likely to leave their jobs after six months to a year. To build a sustainable, inclusive culture, Guillory's team is having remote conversations with people to find out what conditions would make them most inclined to stay with the company longer-term.

The DEI team is also designing ways to connect people when they don't have random run-ins with colleagues, and this is one of the measures they're instituting in a very intentional way. "We're having quarterly social-impact days to bring team members together on a cause, and community activities," Guillory says. With more-blurred boundaries, there's a chance to redesign rituals and personal connections in ways that establish common interests among people from different backgrounds, and to build an intentional culture from the ground up.

What to do: Reimagine the role of remote workspaces when it comes to where you can find talent and how you can build an intentionally diverse, anti-racist workplace culture.

The pressure is on to make technology serve the greater good

We've seen how technology can be a force against inclusion. A 2020 UN report summed up a number of egregious examples. In January of 2020, an African American man in Michigan was arrested for shoplifting and spent several hours in jail before the police realized he was innocent. The police officers had trusted facial-recognition software to identify their suspect—but the technology has been unable in many cases to recognize the differences among Black faces. In July of the same year a computer program in the United Kingdom penalized students from minority and low-income areas, shattering their hopes of getting into universities, because it deducted points for those who had gone to high schools with lower academic ratings.[19] Social-media companies have used AI-powered algorithms to microtarget users and send them tailored content that will reinforce their prejudices. Research from New York University finds that data from the worst-behaving police departments is nevertheless used to inform predictive-policing tools, thus building racist data into AI systems.[20]

Yet we are beginning to see the corporate leaders who understand that they have to police AI itself, along with other advanced technologies, to ensure that the technology of the future propels diversity and inclusion rather than harming it. I like the way a researcher in a video that accompanies the UN report puts it: "Dr. Frankenstein let his creation find its own way into the world, and that's when it became a monster. We will create a monster if we unleash AI without guiding it every step of the way, but if we guide it purposefully and intentionally it can be a force for good."[21]

Danny Guillory has examined the conjunction of diversity, unconscious bias, and artificial intelligence in depth. "Having a software development team that is diverse across multiple dimensions (ethnicity, sex, ability, age, etc.) is essential to ensure that many points of view are truly integrated into the product," he wrote in a LinkedIn commentary. "Integrating diversity into the product development process is a responsibility that as technology companies we should all take as seriously as privacy—and if we embed this thinking early, we will save ourselves from course correcting later on."[22]

What to do: Be very intentional about DEI and anti-racism in the technology that you use and insist upon highly diverse software-development teams in your organization.

Keep an Eye on the Next Generation of Business Leaders

The work I've been doing with business leaders is tremendously rewarding and gives me reasons to be optimistic about the future, but if you were to ask me to name a single source for my optimism, I would, without a moment's hesitation, point to a new generation of young, diverse entrepreneurs who are truly changing the world.

One of the most critical opportunities to reverse systemic racism is through the economic engine that fuels innovation and disruptive growth. Part of my work now involves seeking out people of color who are starting businesses. There are a number of brilliant, innovative entrepreneurs who have been largely overlooked by the venture-capital world because they don't fit the conventional image—that is, they aren't well-connected young white males. I've had the honor and pleasure of working with about half a dozen entrepreneurs of color and their startups. Here is a look at a few such dynamic leaders, who work with diverse networks and ecosystems as a matter of course, and their companies, which have become living proof of how society benefits when everyone has a chance to reach their full potential:

Dr. Lisa Dyson, an African American, MIT-trained physicist who just might have some answers to the world's food-shortage problem, is now running her second biotech startup, Air Protein, which she cofounded in 2019. The company harnesses technology developed by NASA that uses microorganisms to transform fermented carbon dioxide into meat substitutes. Her work has been featured on *NOVA*, the PBS science series. Air Protein has raised $32 million in series-A funding from ADM Ventures, Barclays Ventures, and GV, and the company is valued at $100 million.

Dyson grew up with a father who was an entrepreneur, and she was always a self-described "math and science nerd." In high school, she wanted to learn the programming language C, but there were no classes. So she asked her math teacher to teach her—and he agreed to teach her every day during his free period. She went to fourteen different schools growing up and told me that the experience taught her how powerfully a person's environment can affect the way they perform.

In 2005, a year after earning a PhD in theoretical high-energy physics from MIT, she went to New Orleans to help rebuild after Hurricane Katrina, and that was when she realized she wanted to become part of the solution to climate change.

"In climate change it's always the most disenfranchised people who are affected the most," she says. And ultimately, she wanted to develop climate-friendly food products because the food sector, especially the meat industry, is one of the world's largest sources of greenhouse-gas emissions.

In building her companies, she has incorporated the lessons she learned in school about the importance of a supportive environment. "You have to prioritize culture from the start," she says. "I focus on having high expectations for my team and motivating everyone, motivating them with a goal beyond what they think they can do."[23]

The booming alternative-protein industry is yet another white-male-dominated industry, and Dyson is the only Black woman I know of in this space. She's the fourth Black woman ever to achieve a PhD in theoretical high-energy physics, and one of the first to receive significant venture funding. But she won't be the last.

Alejandro Velez and Nikhil Arora are the founders of Back to the Roots, which makes organic gardening kits for children and is helping bring fresh-grown produce to inner cities. Their big idea for a business began in 2009, when they were both seniors at UC Berkeley. They didn't know each other well, but they were in the same business-ethics class, and both were blown away when their professor, while lecturing on sustainability, mentioned a little-known factoid that it is possible to grow gourmet mushrooms from used coffee grounds. Each of them, separately, asked their professor for more information, and the professor brought them together. Though neither planned to go into science—Arora was studying political science and business, while Velez was majoring in education—they began experimenting with the mushroom-growing process in the kitchen of Velez's fraternity house, and successfully produced their first crop.

They received a $5,000 grant from the school chancellor, and when they graduated, they both decided to forgo the corporate jobs they had lined up and take a chance with a startup. They now have significant financing, led by the venture-capital firms Acre Venture Partners and S2G Ventures, and were among EY's Entrepreneur of the Year 2021 award finalists for the Northern California region.

The company produces a variety of organic gardening starter kits, with seedlings designed to bloom in any environment, including inner-city apartment windows. One of the company's purposeful ideas has been to source its products with independent farmers in the Midwest, many of whom have given up commodity farming, with its economic uncertainties and pesticide requirements, for organic specialty farming. On the company's website Velez and Arora talk about their goal of making food growing and wellness accessible to people everywhere: "We want to help every family and kid across the country experience the magic and wonder of growing their own food—no green thumb or big backyard needed!"

These two young entrepreneurs have also been adamant that there will be no racial marginalization on their watch. They have made a commitment to showing photos of diverse users on all of the company's packages and on the Back to the Roots website. Such details have an important role in delivering the right message within the organization and in society.

Tomorrow's Leaders Will Have a Powerful Impact

In the course of writing this book, I spent a lot of time talking with my daughter Krista about tomorrow's leaders and the future that her generation will shape. "Imagine how business leaders could change the world for both workers and consumers if we shifted the paradigm away from valuing profit to the exclusion of everything else," she said.

We realized that we share an optimistic view of how things could change. In a planet-first paradigm, the future Dr. Lisa Dysons could help solve the climate crisis. In an innovation-first paradigm, the greatest minds of Silicon Valley and beyond could help create more-accessible tech, and AI that works for *good*, fighting against bias and racism that has held back a significant percentage of the population. A community-first paradigm might end hunger or the housing crisis. Other paradigms could center people, empathy, liberation, joy, sovereignty, healing, connection, and more. And an anti-racist-first paradigm creates the conditions for all these other paradigms to exist. Focusing on anti-racism as the foundation of a company lays the groundwork for breaking down barriers in every marginalization. True anti-racism is intersectional.

Working on this project with Krista has left me hopeful that a more equitable workplace is on the horizon. I envision a future of work that looks something like this: people of all races, genders, sexualities,

A Final Checklist

- The future is now!
- A DEI culture is essential if your business is going to remain relevant.
- You have to build an anti-racist company by design.
- Businesses can, and must, be a force for good.
- All stakeholders are demanding change.
- The CEO and the board must lead the transformation.
- The next generation of inclusive leaders is rapidly emerging.

religions, and abilities are promoted on potential, paid equally, given the access and support they need to succeed, and respected in the fullness of their humanity. I think of the words from Lin-Manuel Miranda's great multicultural musical *Hamilton*: "America, you great unfinished symphony, you sent for me. You let me make a difference." We are facing a great unfinished symphony now. As business leaders, we have a unique opportunity to make history, guiding the country to a reality in which capitalism and the American Dream work for *everyone*—and we will all be better off for it.

Resources for Further Learning

My Business Book Reading List

Below is my list of four business books that have taught me never to underestimate the human capacity to do great things.

Doing What Matters: How to Get Results That Make a Difference—the Revolutionary Old-School Approach, by James M. Kilts with John F. Manfredi and Robert L. Lorber, is my favorite guide to management. Kilts, who was my boss at Gillette, has written a leadership playbook that has been instrumental in my practice of putting people and teams into roles that unlock their full potential.

The Leadership Engine: How Winning Companies Build Leaders at Every Level, by Noel M. Tichy with Eli Cohen, has been my guide to helping people in my organization develop as leaders. Tichy, a consultant and professor at the Ross School of Management at the University of Michigan, coined the term "teachable point of view," which is the core of how leaders develop other leaders. A leader, says

Tichy, has a set of ideas, and a set of values to support the ideas, but also needs to be able to motivate others to buy into those ideas and values, and having a teachable point of view enables a leader to make important judgments about people, strategy, and crisis. He believes everyone has untapped leadership potential that can be developed.

The Last Word on Power: Executive Re-invention for Leaders Who Must Make the Impossible Happen, by management consultant Tracy Goss, has done much to shape my views on transforming individuals and making the impossible happen. Goss is adamant that successful business leaders never stop growing; the skills that got you to the top might at some point prove to be constraints that you have to shed to continue to be successful. One of the most important lessons I carry around from this book: "Most executives don't design a winning strategy—it designs you." You've succeeded by doing things a certain way, but you get so accustomed to that strategy that "if you confront something that you can't accomplish through your winning strategy you label it impossible—which is why convention-ally successful engineers in the late 19th century thought manned flight was impossible." She also stresses the importance of really listening to other people, and not "listening for" what your precon-ceived ideas tell you they're going to say.

Play Bigger: How Pirates, Dreamers, and Innovators Create and Dominate Markets, by Al Ramadan, Dave Peterson, Christopher Lochhead, and Kevin Maney, has given me a great deal of inspiration for reinventing the way we think and do business. The authors are founders of a Silicon Valley advisory firm, and the book is about the discipline of category design and how any industry can apply it to change the world, even solving problems we didn't know we had.

More Resources for Understanding Racism

Caste: The Origins of Our Discontents, by Isabel Wilkerson, is my top recommendation, a book every business leader should read for a greater understanding of what systemic racism looks like in America.
Additional recommendations:

- *So You Want to Talk about Race*, by Ijeoma Oluo

- *White Fragility: Why It's So Hard for White People to Talk about Racism*, by Robin DiAngelo

- *Stamped from the Beginning: The Definitive History of Racist Ideas in America*, by Ibram X. Kendi

- *Between the World and Me*, by Ta-Nehisi Coates

- *The New Jim Crow: Mass Incarceration in the Age of Colorblindness*, by Michelle Alexander

- *Just Mercy: A Story of Justice and Redemption*, by Bryan Stevenson

- *13th*, Netflix

- *When They See Us*, Netflix

Peer-Group Resources for Business Leaders

Billion Dollar Roundtable: Recognizes and celebrates corporations that spend at least $1 billion with minority- and women-owned suppliers.

Chief Executives for Corporate Purpose (CECP): A group of 200 CEOs, business leaders, and top executives committed to standing against racism and making structural changes, founded in 1999 by actor and philanthropist Paul Newman and other business leaders.

The Distinguished Careers Institute (DCI) at Stanford: A yearlong residential program of personal renewal and community engagement for business leaders, DCI sponsors a few activities, adjunctive programs, and events that support the exploration of purpose, including colloquiums on important issues such as racial justice and equity. I'm a member of the DCI class of 2018, and I've been particularly pleased to see that the institute now has seventy leaders who are focusing on how the corporate world can achieve greater racial justice and equity.

Great Place to Work: A management-consulting company that is building "for-all" leadership cultures around the world.

The Justice, Equity, Diversity, Inclusion (J.E.D.I.) Collaborative: A collaborative of leaders in the natural-products industry, dedicated to developing greater justice, equity, diversity, and inclusion throughout the industry and the global food ecosystem.

Management Leadership for Tomorrow (MLT): A national organization committed to transforming the corporate-leadership pipeline by empowering people from underrepresented minorities to reach their greatest potential. The MLT works with more than

120 organizations and has a community of more than eight thousand rising leaders.

Multicultural Foodservice & Hospitality Alliance (MFHA):
An industry association that educates members on expanding their "cultural intelligence" to effectively engage multicultural employees, customers, and communities.

Network of Executive Women (NEW): An organization that has brought together more than 13,500 women representing nearly nine hundred organizations across North America. NEW's mission is to advance and empower women leaders as well as to provide insights and practical solutions to help businesses transform through gender equality.

OneTen: A coalition of thirty-seven CEOs with the goal of creating one million new jobs for Black Americans by 2030.

Women's Foodservice Forum (WFF): An organization that partners with food-industry leaders to improve gender diversity at every level. Since its founding in 1989, WFF has provided networking, mentorship, and leadership development for women in the food industry.

XPRIZE Racial Equity Alliance: A global cross-industry collaboration between XPRIZE, a global future positive nonprofit organization, and the Coalition of Black Excellence that seeks to create a more just and equitable society in both the public and private sectors. The group advocates for policy changes and is creating initiatives that will address existing challenges and seek innovative approaches to achieving racial equity.

Resources for Workplace-Experience Audits and Employee-Engagement Signaling

- Gallup, https://www.gallup.com/home.aspx

- Great Place to Work, https://www.greatplacetowork.com/

- Medallia, https://www.medallia.com/

- Survey Monkey, https://www.surveymonkey.com/

Resources for Supporting Workplace Equality and Recruiting Diverse Professionals

- Catalyst: Workplaces That Work for Women, https://www.catalyst.org/

- LEAP (Leadership Education for Asian Pacifics), https://www.leap.org/

- Management Leadership for Tomorrow (MLT): Provides training and networks for Black, Latinx, and Native American executive talent as well as recruitment, retention, and diversity-strategy consulting for businesses, https://mlt.org/

- NAAAP (National Association of Asian American Professionals), https://naaap.org/

- National Black MBA Association (NBMBAA), https://nbmbaa.org/

- Out & Equal (LGBTQIA+ community), https://outandequal .org/

- Prospanica (Hispanic MBAs and business professionals), https://www.prospanica.org/

- Reaching Out (LGBTQIA+ MBA community), https:// reachingoutmba.org/

Notes

Chapter 1

1. Dieter Holger, "The Business Case for More Diversity," *The Wall Street Journal*, October 26, 2019, https://www.wsj.com/articles/the-business-case-for-more-diversity -11572091200; Rocío Lorenzo et al., "How Diverse Leadership Teams Boost Innovation," Boston Consulting Group, January 23, 2018, https://www.bcg.com/en-us/publications /2018/how-diverse-leadership-teams-boost-innovation.aspx.

2. Earl Fitzhugh et al., "It's Time for a New Approach to Racial Equity," McKinsey & Company, December 2, 2020, updated May 25, 2021, https://www.mckinsey.com /featured-insights/diversity-and-inclusion/its-time-for-a-new-approach-to-racial-equity.

3. John Rice, "The Difference between First-Degree Racism and Third-Degree Racism," *The Atlantic*, June 21, 2020, https://www.theatlantic.com/business/archive /2020/06/three-degrees-racism-america/613333/.

4. Bracken Darrell, "I Can't Breathe," LinkedIn, May 29, 2020, https://www .linkedin.com/pulse/i-cant-breathe-bracken-darrell/.

5. Elahe Izadi, "The Incidents That Led to the University of Missouri President's Resignation," *Washington Post*, November 9, 2015, https://www.washingtonpost.com /news/grade-point/wp/2015/11/09/the-incidents-that-led-to-the-university-of-missouri -presidents-resignation/.

6. Cindy Levy et al., "Coronavirus: 15 Emerging Themes for Boards and Executive Teams," McKinsey & Company, June 2, 2020, https://www.mckinsey.com/business -functions/risk/our-insights/coronavirus-15-emerging-themes-for-boards-and-executive -teams.

7. Dana M. Peterson, Catherine L. Mann, and Raymond J. McGuire, "Closing the Racial Inequality Gaps: The Economic Cost of Black Inequality in the U.S.," *Citi GPS: Global Perspectives & Solutions*, September 2020, https://ir.citi.com/NvIUklHPilz14Hwd 3oxqZBLMn1_XPqo5FrxsZD0x6hhil84ZxaxEuJUWmak51UHvYk75VKeHCMI%3D.

8. Nick Noel et al., "The Economic Impact of Closing the Racial Wealth Gap," McKinsey & Company, April 13, 2019, https://www.mckinsey.com/industries/public -sector/our-insights/the-economic-impact-of-closing-the-racial-wealth-gap.

9. Cromwell Schubarth, "Snowflake CEO Frank Slootman Walks Back Remarks about Diversity, Hiring," *Silicon Valley Business Journal*, June 8, 2021, https://www .bizjournals.com/sanjose/news/2021/06/08/snowflake-ceo-walks-back-remarks-about -diversity.html.

10. Peter Senge, *The Fifth Discipline: The Art and Practice of the Learning Organization* (Crown Business, New York, 2006), 227, e-book edition. Originally published by Doubleday Group, Inc., 1990.

11. Todd Schnuck, video call with author, February 9, 2021.

12. Paul Feinberg, "Stand Up and Speak Out," UCLA Anderson School of Management: News and Events, June 19, 2019, https://www.anderson.ucla.edu/news-and-events/stand-up-and-speak-out.

Chapter 2

1. Joan C. Williams and James D. White, "Update Your DE&I Playbook," *Harvard Business Review*, July 15, 2020, https://hbr.org/2020/07/update-your-dei-playbook?ab=hero-main-text.

2. Tyler Clifford, "Nielsen CEO Explains Why He Took on the Additional Role of Chief Diversity Officer," CNBC.com, June 19, 2020, https://www.cnbc.com/2020/06/19/white-nielsen-ceo-explains-decision-to-become-chief-diversity-officer.html.

3. Lianna Brinded, "Nielsen CEO and Chief Diversity Officer: How to Be an Advocate and Transform Your Business by Embedding D&I," Yahoo Finance UK, June 17, 2020, https://uk.finance.yahoo.com/news/nielsen-ceo-chief-diversity-officer-david-kenny-how-to-be-advocate-diversity-inclusion-empower-230154077.html.

4. Khadeeja Safdar and Keach Hagey, "Black Executives Are Sharing Their Experiences of Racism, Many for the First Time," *The Wall Street Journal*, June 26, 2020, https://www.wsj.com/articles/black-executives-are-sharing-their-experiences-of-racism-many-for-the-first-time-11593182200.

5. Brian Cornell, "A Note from Brian Cornell to Our Teams and Communities in the Twin Cities and Beyond," Target, May 29, 2020, https://corporate.target.com/article/2020/05/supporting-communities-minnesota-beyond.

6. Clifton Leaf and Bernard J. Tyson, "How Diversity Can Improve the Healthcare Experience with Bernard J. Tyson, Kaiser Permanente," Great Place to Work for All Summit, 2019, https://www.greatplacetowork.com/forallsummit/keynotes/how-diversity-can-improve-the-healthcare-experience-with-bernard-j-tyson-kaiser-permanente.

7. Jason Wingard, "Bernard Tyson: Lessons from a Great American CEO," *Forbes*, November 15, 2019, https://www.forbes.com/sites/jasonwingard/2019/11/15/bernard-tyson-lessons-from-a-great-american-leader/#37aaede943a4.

8. "The Future of Healthcare with the Late Bernard Tyson, Former Chairman & CEO, Kaiser Permanente," *Pivot to the Future* (podcast), October 2019, https://open.spotify.com/episode/6KVSFouySex9vMurbc7mDv?si=Y9_osfd5RGyEFrqae_FFFg.

9. "A Message from Chairman and CEO Lisa Wardell: George Floyd Tragedy," Adtalem Global Education, May 31, 2020, https://www.adtalem.com/newsroom/articles/a-message-from-chairman-and-ceo-lisa-wardell-george-floyd-tragedy.

Chapter 3

1. Lisa Wardell, video call with author, January 11, 2021.

2. Larry Ruff, video call with author, February 2, 2021.

3. "Starbucks Executive Weighs in on Arrests of 2 Black Men," *Morning Edition*, National Public Radio, April 16, 2018, https://www.npr.org/2018/04/16/602807632/starbucks-executive-weighs-in-on-arrests-of-2-black-men.

4. Wardell, video call with author, January 11, 2021.

5. "2020 Global Board Diversity Tracker," Egon Zehnder, https://www
.egonzehnder.com/global-board-diversity-tracker.

6. "Data USA: Food Preparation Workers," Data USA, https://datausa.io/profile
/soc/food-preparation-workers#demographics.

7. Bracken Darrell, "Logitech: Defy(ing) the Logic of the Past," March 2021,
https://s1.q4cdn.com/104539020/files/doc_downloads/2021/Logitech-Strategy-and
-Outlook-AID-2021.pdf.

8. Black Enterprise Editors, "Target's Laysha Ward Can't Rest Until Systemic
Racism Is Dismantled," Black Enterprise, June 29, 2020, https://www.blackenterprise
.com/portraits-of-power-laysha-ward/?test=prebid.

9. "Target Releases Workforce Diversity Report; Plans to Increase Representation
of Black Team Members across the Company by 20 Percent over Three Years," Target
press release, September 10, 2020, https://corporate.target.com/press/releases/2020/09
/target-releases-workforce-diversity-report-plans-t.

10. Jackie Krentzman, "From Floor to Ceiling," DiversityWomanMedia, March 26,
2021, https://www.diversitywoman.com/from-floor-to-ceiling/.

11. Imani Moise, Jessica DiNapoli, and Ross Kerber, "Exclusive: Wells Fargo
CEO Ruffles Feathers with Comments about Diverse Talent," Reuters, September 22, 2020, https://www.reuters.com/article/us-global-race-wells-fargo-exclusive
/exclusive-wells-fargo-ceo-ruffles-feathers-with-comments-about-diverse-talent
-idUSKCN26D2IU.

12. "What Is Action Learning?" World Institute for Action Learning, https://wial
.org/action-learning/.

13. Noel M. Tichy, The Leadership Engine: How Winning Companies Build Leaders at
Every Level (New York: HarperBusiness Essentials, 1997), 4.

14. Joan C. Williams and James D. White, "Update Your DE&I Playbook," Harvard
Business Review, July 15, 2020, https://hbr.org/2020/07/update-your-dei-playbook.

15. Mike Fuccillo, video call with author, December 21, 2020.

16. Future of Fitness virtual event, Club Industry, March 9, 2021, https://futureoffitness
.clubindustry.com/futureoffitnessclubin/march-demand.

Chapter 4

1. Leslie Stretch, "The Medallia Commitment," 13for13, June 9, 2020, https://www
.13for13.org/medallia-ceo-pledge.

2. Leslie Stretch, video call with author, July 7, 2021.

3. "Tyson Food Managers Bet on Workers Getting Covid-19, Lawsuit Says," BBC
News, November 19, 2020, https://www.bbc.com/news/world-us-canada-55009228.

4. Erby Foster, video call with author, December 29, 2020.

5. "The Clorox Acquires Soy Vay Enterprises," M&A Deal Summary, December 2011, https://mergr.com/the-clorox-acquires-soy-vay-enterprises.

6. Deborah Ashton, video call with author, February 2, 2021.

7. Lisa Wardell, video call with author, January 11, 2021.

8. Janice Duis, video call with author, December 21, 2020.

9. Bernard J. Tyson, interviewed by Paul Michelman, "The Question Every
Executive Should Ask," MIT Sloan Management Review, Summer 2017, https://sloanreview
.mit.edu/article/the-question-every-executive-should-ask/.

Notes

10. "Did You Know: Model Minority Myth," Asians@Twilio, May 13, 2021, https://www.youtube.com/watch?v=NWnJDFpOaVQ.

11. Joan C. Williams and James D. White, "Update Your DE&I Playbook," *Harvard Business Review*, July 15, 2020, https://hbr.org/2020/07/update-your-dei-playbook.

12. Kathryn Mayer, "HR's Mandate to Model Diversity and Inclusion," *Human Resource Executive*, August 12, 2020, https://hrexecutive.com/hrs-mandate-to-model-diversity-and-inclusion.

13. Ragini Holloway, "Lead by Example and Build a Diverse Team," LinkedIn, May 1, 2019, https://www.linkedin.com/pulse/lead-example-build-diverse-team-ragini-holloway/.

14. Ibid.

15. Ibid.

16. Danielle Gaucher, Justin Friesen, and Aaron C. Kay, "Evidence That Gendered Wording in Job Advertisements Exists and Sustains Gender Inequality," *Journal of Personality and Social Psychology* 101, no. 1 (2011): 109.

Chapter 5

1. Michael Bush and Christopher Tkaczyk, "Why 2020 Marks the Era of the 'For All' Leader," *Fortune*, February 18, 2020, https://fortune.com/2020/02/18/100-best-companies-2020-for-all-leader/.

2. Behnam Tabrizi, "The Key to Change Is Middle Management," *Harvard Business Review*, October 27, 2014, https://hbr.org/2014/10/the-key-to-change-is-middle-management.

3. Lisa Wardell, video call with author, January 11, 2021.

4. Michael C. Bush, *A Great Place to Work for All* (Oakland, CA: Berrett-Koehler, 2018).

5. Dnika J. Travis, Emily Shaffer, and Jennifer Thorpe-Moscon, "Getting Real about Inclusive Leadership: Why Change Starts with You," Catalyst, 2020, https://www.catalyst.org/wp-content/uploads/2020/03/Getting-Real-About-Inclusive-Leadership-Report-2020update.pdf.

6. Roxanne Jones, "Kamala Harris Shows Black Women They Have the Power to Change the World," CNN, November 10, 2020, https://www.cnn.com/2020/11/10/opinions/kamala-harris-black-women-jones/index.html.

7. Wardell, video call with author, January 11, 2021.

8. "Bias Interrupters: Small Steps, Big Change," The Center for WorkLife Law, UC Hastings College of the Law, https://biasinterrupters.org/.

9. Joan C. Williams and James D. White, "Update Your DE&I Playbook," *Harvard Business Review*, July 15, 2020, https://hbr.org/2020/07/update-your-dei-playbook.

10. Kate Conger, "Hundreds of Google Employees Unionize, Culminating Years of Activism," *New York Times*, January 4, 2021, https://www.nytimes.com/2021/01/04/technology/google-employees-union.html.

11. Erby Foster, video call with author, December 29, 2020.

Chapter 6

1. Bryan Stevenson, "The Power of Proximity," CEO Initiative 2018, *Fortune*, June 27, 2018, https://www.youtube.com/watch?v=1RyAwZIHo4Y.

2. "Leadership in Action," Business Roundtable, https://www.businessroundtable.org/.

3. *Oxford Essential Quotations*, 2nd ed. (Oxford: Oxford University Press, 2017), https://www.oxfordreference.com/view/10.1093/acref/9780191843730.001.0001/q-oro-ed5-00016497.

4. Alex Abad-Santos, "Nike's Colin Kaepernick Ad Sparked a Boycott—and Earned $6 Billion for Nike," *Vox*, September 24, 2018, https://www.vox.com/2018/9/24/17895704/nike-colin-kaepernick-boycott-6-billion.

5. Jennifer Strailey, "All In: How Walmart, Albertsons and Target Are Accelerating Change," *Winsight Grocery Business*, February 8, 2021, https://www.winsightgrocerybusiness.com/retailers/all-how-walmart-albertsons-target-are-accelerating-change.

6. Clifton Leaf and Bernard J. Tyson, "How Diversity Can Improve the Healthcare Experience with Bernard J. Tyson, Kaiser Permanente," Great Place to Work for All Summit, 2019, https://www.greatplacetowork.com/forallsummit/keynotes/how-diversity-can-improve-the-healthcare-experience-with-bernard-j-tyson-kaiser-permanente.

7. Report from Target to Business Roundtable, 2021, https://www.businessroundtable.org/policy-perspectives/diversity/target

8. "Supplier Diversity," Target, https://corporate.target.com/about/products-services/suppliers/supplier-diversity.

9. "2020 Supplier Diversity Impact Report," CVS Health, https://cvshealth.com/sites/default/files/cvs-health-supplier-diversity-impact-report-2020.pdf; "2019 Supplier Diversity Economic Impact Report," PG&E, https://www.pge.com/pge_global/common/pdfs/for-our-business-partners/purchasing-program/suppliers/supply-chain-responsibility/2019-Supplier-Diversity-Economic-Impact-Report.pdf; "TIAA Economic Impact Report 2019," TIAA, https://www.tiaa.org/public/pdf/2019-supplier-diversity-economic-impact-report.pdf.

10. David Sarokin and Jay Schulkin, *The Corporation: Its History and Future* (Newcastle upon Tyne: Cambridge Scholars Publishing, 2020), 148.

11. Abhinav Singh, "Underpayment, Exploitation: Luxury Brand Zara's Racism against Its Own Workers Is out in the Open," TFIPost, May 9, 2020, https://tfipost.com/2020/05/underpayment-exploitation-luxury-brand-zaras-racism-against-its-own-workers-is-out-in-the-open/.

12. John Nanry, "The US Needs a National Guard for Manufacturing," *Industry-Week*, January 27, 2021, https://www.industryweek.com/covid19/article/21153483/the-us-needs-a-national-manufacturing-guard.

13. Alexis Bateman, Ashley Barrington, and Katie Date, "Why You Need a Supplier-Diversity Program," *Harvard Business Review*, August 17, 2020, https://hbr.org/2020/08/why-you-need-a-supplier-diversity-program.

14. Melanie Curtin, "73 Percent of Millennials Are Willing to Spend More Money on This 1 Type of Product," *Inc.*, March 30, 2018, https://www.inc.com/melanie-curtin/73-percent-of-millennials-are-willing-to-spend-more-money-on-this-1-type-of-product.html.

Chapter 7

1. Amanda Gorman, *The Hill We Climb: An Inaugural Poem for the Country* (New York: Viking, 2021).

2. "S&P 500 Racial Justice and DEI Scorecard Separates Leaders from Laggards," As You Sow, March 4, 2021, https://www.asyousow.org/press-releases/2021/3/3/racial -justice-dei-scorecard-leaders-laggards.

3. Sidney Fussell, "Black Tech Employees Rebel against 'Diversity Theater,'" *Wired*, March 8, 2021, https://www.wired.com/story/black-tech-employees-rebel -against-diversity-theater/.

4. Ibid.

5. Nikhil Bumb, Chris Carlson, and Lakshmi Iyer, "Change the World—for Whom? Why Addressing Racism Must Be a Top Corporate Priority," *Fortune*, September 21, 2020, https://fortune.com/2020/09/21/change-the-world-companies-must-tackle -racism.

6. "Corporate Governance: Long-Term Value Creation," Business Roundtable, https://www.businessroundtable.org/policy-perspectives/corporate-governance/long -term-value-creation.

7. Stanford GSB, "Rosalind Brewer: Find Your Voice and Don't Be Silent," *View from the Top* (podcast), June 23, 2021, https://www.gsb.stanford.edu/insights/rosalind -brewer-find-your-voice-dont-be-silent.

8. "Rosalind Brewer: COO and Group President, Starbucks," Talks at GS, March 14, 2019, https://www.youtube.com/watch?v=wW8cPtt8xo0.

9. Ezra Klein, "Ibram X. Kendi Wants to Redefine Racism," *Vox Conversations* (podcast), 2019, https://podcasts.apple.com/us/podcast/ibram-x-kendi-wants-to-redefine -racism/id1081584611?i=1000452609664.

10. Spencer Stuart S&P MidCap 400 Board Report, Spencer Stuart, https://www .spencerstuart.com/-/media/2021/january/midcap/sp_midcap_400_report.pdf.

11. Ben Eisen, "Goldman Sachs Unveils $10 Billion Push to Invest in Black Women," *Wall Street Journal*, March 10, 2021, https://www.wsj.com/articles/goldman-sachs -unveils-10-billion-push-to-invest-in-black-women-11615394850.

12. "Access to Capital for Minority-Owned Businesses," US Chamber of Commerce, https://www.uschamber.com/sites/default/files/ccmc_growthengine_accesstocapital .pdf.

13. James Fontanella-Khan and Michael Mackenzie, "Ariel and JPMorgan to Invest in Minority-Owned Companies," *Financial Times*, February 17, 2021, https://www.ft .com/content/256375ca-2858-43d8-99c9-48ee21900e82.

14. Two examples are Richard Branson, "Thoughts on America," Richard Branson's blog, January 15, 2021, https://www.virgin.com/branson-family/richard-branson-blog /thoughts-on-america; Dropbox Team, "Truth and Reconciliation: How Dropbox Is Supporting the Black Lives Matter Movement," Inside DBX (blog), October 2, 2020, https://blog.dropbox.com/topics/inside-dbx/truth-and-reconciliation--how-dropbox-is -supporting-the-black-li.

15. John Gittelsohn, "Realtors Apologize for Role in Housing Racial Discrimination," *Bloomberg*, November 19, 2020, https://www.bloomberg.com/news/articles/2020 -11-19/realtors-apologize-for-role-in-housing-racial-discrimination.

16. Harry McCracken, "Why We're Entering a Significant Moment in the Fight for Equity in Tech," *Fast Company*, June 16, 2021, https://www.fastcompany.com/90643516 /ken-chenault-black-in-tech-equity-fight.

17. Julie Washington, video call with author, January 30, 2021.

18. Danny Guillory, video call with author, February 3, 2021.

19. "Bias, Racism and Lies: Facing Up to the Unwanted Consequences of AI," *UN News*, December 30, 2020, https://news.un.org/en/story/2020/12/1080192.

20. Rashida Richardson, Jason Schultz, and Kate Crawford, "Dirty Data, Bad Predictions: How Civil Rights Violations Impact Police Data, Predictive Policing Systems, and Justice," *New York University Law Review* 94, no. 192 (2019): 192–233, https://papers.ssrn.com/sol3/papers.cfm?abstract_id=3333423.

21. "Bias, Racism and Lies," *UN News*.

22. Danny Guillory, "Building Diversity into Artificial Intelligence Software Development," LinkedIn.com, January 26, 2021, https://www.linkedin.com/pulse/building-diversity-artificial-intelligence-software-danny-guillory/.

23. Lisa Dyson, video call with author, July 1, 2021.

Index

accountability, 51

action learning, 87–88, 183–185

action-learning teams (ALTs), 70, 87–91
 at Clorox, 102–105
 in design for change, 100–106
 at Jamba Juice, 41–42, 43–44
 middle managers in, 138–139

action plans, 70, 75, 91–93, 98, 117

Adams, Greg, 55

Adidas, 158

Adtalem Global Education, 10, 56–58
 Covid-19 pandemic and, 153–154
 middle managers at, 128–129
 speaking out about bias at, 107–108

affinity groups, 31–32

Affirm, 119–120

Air Protein, 190

alignment, 76–78

allyship, 132

Amyris, Inc., 27

anti-racism, 172, 177
 conscious capital for, 178–180
 resources for, 196–201
 societal benefits of, 173

anti-racist-first paradigm, 192–193

apartheid, 97, 180

Arbery, Ahmaud, 4

Ariel Investments, 179–180

Arnold, Craig, 172

Arora, Nikhil, 191–192

artificial intelligence (AI), biases in, 121, 187–189

Ashton, Deborah, 105–106

assignments, 115, 137–140

As You Sow, 172

audit, workplace-experience, 200

audits, cultural, 40, 70, 79–82, 116
 documenting your current state and, 70, 82–85

Aunt Jemima, 152–153

authenticity, 74, 149

authority
 to change culture, 48–50
 decision-making, 129–130

Back to the Roots, 191–192

Banks, Aerica Shimizu, 172–173

Bay Club Company, 91, 112–113

Benchmark, 37

benchmarks, 70, 85–87, 116

Berrard, Steven, 36, 37

bias
 in AI, 121, 187–189
 emotional tax of, 26
 identifying, 139–140
 interrupting, 134–137, 138, 139–144
 ladder of inference and, 109–111
 learning to see your own, 116–117, 139–140
 in performance reviews, 142–143
 in seeing potential, 25–26
 speaking out when you see, 107–108, 132
 stamping out at the source, 148–149
 unconscious, 25–26
 unconscious, overcoming, 43

Biden, Joe, 171

Billion Dollar Roundtable, 197

biodiversity, 20–21

Black Entertainment Television, 56

Black Lives Matter movement, 3–4, 7–8
 in the mainstream, 170
 Medallia and, 59–60
 origins of, 15–16

Black Lives Matter movement (*continued*)
Schnuck Markets and, 23–24
Starbucks and, 68–70
Target and, 13–14
boards of directors, 22, 57, 77–78
bounceback, 142–143
brainstorming, 106
Brewer, Rosalind, 69, 172, 175–176
Brigham Young University, 15–16
Brooks, Rayshard, 4
Brown, Michael, 15, 54, 68–69
burning platform, 23
Burt's Bees Rainbow Pride Lip Balm
Pack, 105
Bush, Michael C., 26, 125–126
business case for diversity, 8–9, 176
getting alignment with, 76–77
supply chain, 156–162
Business Roundtable, 151, 174–175
Butler, Jonathan, 15–16
Byrne, Tom, 36

capital, 178–180
capitalism
discrimination and, 19
systemic racism in, 1
career development, 26–27, 117–124
#CareForCaregivers campaign, 153–154
Carnival Corp., 172
Cartwright, Alexander, 15–16
Caste: The Origins of Our Discontents
(Wilkerson), 72, 197
Catalyst, 26, 131–132
CDOs. *See* chief diversity officers (CDOs)
Center for WorkLife Law, 80, 135–136
Centers for Disease Control and
Prevention (CDC), 12–13
Chamberlain University, 57
Chambers, John, 129
change, 174–189
action learning and, 183–185
action-learning principles in, 100–106
action-learning teams in, 70, 87–91
action plans and, 70, 91–93
benchmarks for, 70, 85–87
burning platform for, 23

buy-in to, 76
catalysts for, 127–130
checklist for CEOs on, 94
communicating expectations for,
130–137
culture audits and, 70, 79–82
documenting the state of your
organization and, 70, 82–85
empathy and, 63–70
getting started with, 63–94
industry peers in, 181–183
intentional communication strategy
and, 100, 106–114
leadership in, 98–99, 100, 115–117
listening and learning in, 70–75
optimism about, 174–175
public profile of, 81–82
pull *vs.* push in, 103–104
resistance to, 144
senior leadership team in, 70, 76–78
steps in, 70
sustainable, 127–130
technology and the greater good, 187–189
time frame for, 78, 137–145
tough conversations and, 180
change management theory, 20
Chauvin, Derek, 7–8
checklist for CEOs, 61, 94, 124, 146, 166
Chenault, Ken, 181–182
chief diversity officers (CDOs), 48–50
authority of, 48–50
at Clorox, 102–105
Chief Executives for Corporate Purpose,
198
Cisco, 129
Citigroup, 19
climate change, 174, 190–191, 192–193
Clorox Company, 102–105, 132–133,
143–144
Coca-Cola, 8, 59–60, 163
"coffee chats," 112–113
Cohen, Eli, 195
commitment
in action plans, 93
to DEI, 73–74
financial, 13–15, 97
to supplier diversity, 160–161

Commonwealth Games, 97
communication
    of action plans, 93
    bias awareness and, 139–140
    of change efforts, 81–82
    empathy and, 66–67
    encouraging openness and, 111–112
    engagement and, skills for, 108–113
    of expectations, 130–137
    intentional strategy for, 100, 106–114
    listening in, 26–27, 52–53
    race and perception in, 175–176
    tough conversations, 180
    visual, 113–114
compensation, tying to DEI, 51, 77, 142,
    144–145
competitive edge, 155–162
conscious capital, 178–180
Cook, Amber, 112–113
Cook, Lloyd, 112–113
Cooper, Amy, 11–12
Cooper, Christian, 11–12
Cornell, Brian, 13–14, 52–53, 83–84,
    155–156, 176
Corporate Equality Index, 50
Covid-19 pandemic, 3–4
    Adtalem and, 57–58, 153–154
    Black Lives Matter and, 7–8
    corporate culture and, 17–18, 51–60
    meatpacking industry in, 19–20, 99
    supply-chain resilience in, 159
    testing inequality in, 12–13, 184–185
    Trump and, 17
    unequal impact of, 170
    workplace change during, 169–170
creativity, 151
culture, 169–191
    auditing, 40, 79–82
    beginning to change, 63–94
    of caring, 14
    CEO investment in, 47–51
    connecting with past, 113–114
    Covid-19 and, 17–18, 51–60
    crisis response and, 58–60
    "eat what you kill" *vs.* "we hunt as a
        pack," 17–18
    enhancing with diversity, 21–22

    generational differences and, 176–177
    inclusive, 16–17, 31–32
    integrating two different, 108–113
    at Jamba Juice, 36, 38–42, 44–47
    as legacy of leaders, 55
    metrics and, 141
    people strategy and, 100, 117–124
    pipeline development for, 105–106,
        143–144
    power of, 19–20
    process for creating, 29
    symbols, rituals, rewards, and, 107
    time frame for changing, 169–170
    transforming, 22–28, 95–124
    virtual-first, 186–187
    virtual workplaces and, 186–187
    visual communication of, 113–114
culture, organizational, 2
    hiring for fit with, 2, 9–10
Culture Amp, 17–18, 22
Culture Design Lab, 3–4, 126–127
Culture First conference, 22
customer base, broadening, 156–157
CVS Health, 157

Darden Restaurants, 105–106
Darrell, Bracken, 14, 81, 160–161
data, 120, 131
Davis, Warner, 29
decision-making
    inclusion in, 16
    middle managers and, 129–130
DEI. *See* diversity, equity, and inclusion
    (DEI)
demographics, 2, 10, 95, 159
Department of Labor's Job Corps
    program, 45
DeVry Education Group, 56
Dickinson, Lara, 20–21
"Did You Know?," 113
Directors Academy, 10
Disability Equality Index, 50
discomfort, getting comfortable with,
    132, 151
dissent, 108
Distinguished Careers Institute, 198

Index

diversity, equity, and inclusion (DEI), 1–2
  barriers to, 99
  business case for, 8–9
  as a business unit, 102–105
  CEO responsibility for, 47–51
  challenges in creating, 9–10
  commitment to, 73–74
  definition of, 16, 54
  diversity theater and, 172–173
  ecosystems for, 147–167
  at every level, 126–127
  financial commitments to, 13–15
  hope and momentum in, 170–172
  integrating into everything, 98
  at Jamba Juice, 38–39
  making a priority, 42–43
  metrics for, 140–144
  misunderstandings about, 9
  openness and, 31–32
  opportunity creation with, 3
  as performance engine, 98
  representation *vs.*, 43
  resilience from, 16–22
  resistance to, 9–10
  resources for, 196–201
  supply chain, 22
  sustainability and, 20–21
  urgency of, 10–16
Dixon, Bea, 156
documentation, 70, 82–85
Doing What Matters (Kilts, Manfredi & Lorber), 195
Donald, Arnold, 172
Dropbox, 186–187
Duis, Janice, 109–112, 113–114
Dyson, Lisa, 189–191, 192–193

Eaton Corp., 172
economic growth, 19, 151, 157
ecosystems, 147–167
  building diversity in, 162–165
  checklist for CEOs on, 166–167
  competitive edge through diverse, 155–162
  economic impact and, 157–158
  empathy, action, and impact in, 152–155
  importance of inclusive, 149–151

  reputational risk and, 158
  resilience and, 159–162
  taking the lead in building, 165–166
efficiency, 18
Egon Zehnder, 78
Ellison, Marvin, 172
Elzinga, Didier, 17–18
emotional tax, 26
empathy, 63–70, 145
  impact and, 152–155
  ladder of inference and, 109–111
  learning, 64–65
  listening and, 66, 67
  modeling, 65–66, 116
  policies and programs for, 67–69
employee engagement surveys, 79–80
employee resource groups (ERGs), 31, 102–105. *See also* affinity groups
  sponsors for, 144
engagement
  of middle management, 130
  resources for measuring, 200
  skills for, 108–113
Enrico, Roger, 88
entrepreneurs, 179–180, 189–191
environmental, social, and corporate governance (ESG) principles, 178–179
Equal Justice Initiative, 150
equity. *See* diversity, equity, and inclusion (DEI)
ethnicity, psychological safety and, 26
expectations, 46–47, 99, 130–137
  interrupting bias and, 135–136

facial-recognition software, 187–188
Fair Housing Act of 1968, 181
Fair Trade USA, 163–164
Fast Radius, 159
fear, 91, 123, 129
Ferguson, Missouri, 15, 68–69
The Fifth Discipline (Senge), 109
financial crisis of 2008–2009, 17
  Jamba Juice and, 35–39
  unemployment in, 147–148
Floyd, George, 4, 7–8, 10–11, 95, 172
Foley, John, 14–15
food access, 182–183, 189–192

"for-all" leaders, 13, 126
Fortune CEO initiative, 149–151
Foster, Erby, 102–105, 133, 143–144
Franklin Templeton, 11–12
Frazier, Darnella, 7
Frazier, Ken, 181
Friedman, Milton, 13
frontline workers, 170
   meatpacking industry, 19–20, 99
Fuccillo, Mike, 90
Fuse Advertising, 101–102

Gallup Q^{12} Employee Engagement
   Survey, 47, 80, 144
Gartner, 185
GE, 88, 104
Gebru, Timnit, 141
GE Leadership Center, 41
Generation Z, 9, 176–177
Georgia State University, 163
Gillette, 11, 27, 30, 64
   growing new markets at, 101
Girls Incorporated of St. Louis, 30
Global Board Diversity Tracker, 78
Global Education Foundation, 57–58
goals, 77–78
   action-learning principles and,
      100–106
   action plans and, 92–93
   benchmarks for, 70, 85–87
   growing new markets, 101–102
   making DEI a business unit, 102–105
   quarterly, 92–93
Goldberg's department store, 96–97
Goldman Sachs, 179
Google, 141
Gorman, Amanda, 170–171
Goss, Tracy, 196
Graham, Stedman, 148
Great Place to Work, 26, 125–126, 198
Great Place to Work for All summit, 155
gross domestic product, 19
Guillory, Danny, 186–187, 188

Hall, Lili, 157
Hamilton (Miranda), 194

Harley-Davidson, 105–106
Harmon, Thomas, 157
Harris, Kamala, 134
health, 182–183
"The Hill We Climb" (Gorman), 170–171
hiring and recruiting
   for cultural fit, 2, 9–10
   DEI, merit, and, 21–22
   documenting current practices in, 82–83
   finding diverse talent and, 64–65
   high potentials, 25
   at historically Black colleges and
      universities, 60
   interrupting bias in, 135–136, 142–144
   interviewing skills and, 122
   at Jamba Juice, 45–46
   at Medallia, 95–96
   performance reviews and, 140–142
   pipeline development for, 105–106
   for potential, 24–26
   resources for, 200–201
   re-spec'ing jobs and, 182
   for transformation, 78
   unbiasing HR and, 117–124
   at Wells Fargo, 84
Holloway, Ragini, 119–120
Howland, MaryAnne, 20–21
"How to Make a Non-Racist Breakfast,"
   152
HR. *See* human resources (HR)
human resources (HR)
   CDOs and, 49
   dismantling structural bias in, 115–116
   people strategy and, 100, 117–124
   power of, 118
Human Rights Campaign (HRC)
   Foundation, 50, 55
humility, 132

incentives, 51, 77, 115, 144
   HR and, 122–123
   at Medallia, 96
inclusion. *See* diversity, equity, and
   inclusion (DEI)
inclusive leadership, 117, 125–146
   definition of, 125
   importance of, 125

Index

Inditex, 158–159
industry organizations, 163–165
innovation, 47, 151, 189–191
interviewing skills, 122

Jamba Juice, 8, 27, 34
  action-learning teams at, 90–91
  brand and potential at, 38–42
  catalysts for change at, 117
  CDO at, 49
  compensation at, 142
  cultural transformation at, 38–42,
    44–47, 114
  culture at, 43
  financial problems at, 35–39
  incentive system at, 144
  listening at, 73
  purpose at, 38–39
  unemployment program at, 147–148
J.E.D.I. *See* Justice, Equity, Diversity,
  Inclusion (J.E.D.I.) Collaborative
Jim Crow laws, 60
job evaluations, 32–33
Johnson, Kevin, 69, 70
Johnson, Robert, 56
Jones, Cheryl, 30
Jones, René, 172
Jones, Roxanne, 134
JPMorgan Chase, 179–180
Juice Club, 36–37
Juneteenth, 96
Justice, Equity, Diversity, Inclusion
  (J.E.D.I.) Collaborative, 20–21,
  76–77, 165, 182–183, 198

Kaepernick, Colin, 153
Kagle, Bob, 37
Kaiser Permanente, 29, 53–55, 112, 154–155
Kanter, Rosabeth Moss, 20
Kellison, Blair, 77
Kenny, David, 50–51
Kilts, Jim, 30, 101, 195
King, Martin Luther Jr., 70, 184
Knauss, Donald, 102
KNOCK, inc., 157
Ku Klux Klan, 59–60

ladder of inference, 109–111
The Last Word on Power (Goss), 196
LatinWorks, 101–102
leaders and leadership
  action-learning teams and, 89–90
  CEO responsibility for DEI and,
    47–51
  in change, 98–99, 174–176
  as change catalysts, 100, 115–117
  communication strategy for, 100,
    106–114
  developing, 129–130
  diversity in, 45–46
  in driving change, 35–61
  empathy and, 63–70
  enlisting and aligning in transforma-
    tions, 70, 76–78
  expectations and, 130–137
  for-all, 13, 126
  importance of anti-racist, 1–2
  inclusive, 117, 125–146
  intentional, 7–34
  learning to lead and, 29–34
  listening and, 26–27, 70–75
  next generation of, 189–191
  power of, 2, 174–175
  promoting underrepresented groups
    and, 133–134
  qualities of intentional, 28
  in transformation, 22–28
The Leadership Engine (Tichy), 41, 88,
  195–196
Leaf, Clifton, 54
learning, focus on, 132
learning organizations, 109–111
"left-hand column," 111–112
Letter from a Birmingham Jail (King), 184
Levchin, Max, 119
Levi's, 66–67
LGBTQIA+ people, psychological safety
  and, 26
Lincoln, Abraham, 97
listening, 26–27, 52–53
  active, 70–75
  empathy and, 66, 67
  questions and, 74–75
  to stakeholders, 40
Lochhead, Christopher, 196–197

Logitech, 14, 81, 160–161
Lorber, Robert L., 195
Lowe's, 172
Lundy, Shontay, 156
Lynch, Tom, 178

Management Leadership for Tomorrow
    (MLT), 12–13, 198–199
Maney, Kevin, 196–197
Manfredi, John F., 195
Marineau, Philip, 66–67
markets, growing new, 101–102
Martin-Busutil, Ramon, 36
Mast, Carlotta, 20–21
McDade, Tony, 4
McDonald's, 145
McKean, Todd, 158
McKinsey, 10, 18, 19
McMillon, Doug, 154
meatpacking industry, 19–20, 99
Medallia, 10, 59–60, 145
    buy-in and alignment at, 77
    culture transformation plan at, 95–98
    empathy at, 67
Medtronic, 105–106
mentoring, 26–27, 163
meritocracy, 8–9, 21–22, 121
metrics, 70, 85–87, 140–144
    tying compensation to, 144–145
middle-level managers
    in action-learning teams, 90, 138–139
    as catalysts for change, 126–130
    communicating expectations for,
        130–137
    in culture change, 46–47
    enlisting in transformation, 76
    high-profile assignments and, 42
    in interrupting bias, 134–137, 138,
        140–144
    time frame for change and, 137–145
millennials, 9, 176–177
Mill Road Capital Management, 178
Minute Maid, 59
Miranda, Lin-Manuel, 194
mission statements, 79
MLT. See Management Leadership for
    Tomorrow (MLT)

modeling, 23
    empathy, 65–66, 116
    inclusive leadership, 145
    intentional leadership, 48
model minority myth, 113
momentum, 172
M&T Bank Corp., 172
Multicultural Foodservice & Hospitality
    Alliance, 199

Nabisco, 101
Nanry, John, 159
NASCAR, 27
National Association of Realtors, 181
National Minority Supplier Development
    Council, 157, 163
Nestlé Purina, 64, 65, 108–113, 133–134
Network of Executive Women, 199
New River Capital, 36
Nielsen, 50–51, 164
Nike, 153, 158
Novant Health, 105–106

Obama, Barack, 134, 147
obsolescence, 18–19, 176–177
O'Loughlin, Sheryl, 20–21
Oluo, Ijeoma, 77, 172
OneTen, 170, 181–182, 199
O Organics, 38
Oppler, Charlie, 181
opportunity
    creating for all, 3
    providing, 32–33
organizational structure, 126–127
    empathy supported by, 66–69

Pacific Gas and Electric, 157
Pearl Milling Company, 152
Peloton, 14–15
Pemberton, Steve, 118–119
people strategy, 100, 117–124
PepsiCo, 88, 152–153
performance
    biased lenses and, 25–26
    DEI as engine of, 98

performance (*continued*)
    evaluations of, 32–33, 139–140
    at Jamba Juice, 38–40
    setting expectations for, 46–47
Perron, Kirk, 36–37, 44, 114
perspective, 109. *See also* empathy
Peterson, Dave, 196–197
Phillips, Charles, 181
pipeline development, 105–106, 143–144,
    162–163
Pivot to the Future podcast, 55
Planet Perspective, 106
Play Bigger (Ramadan, Peterson, Loch-
    head & Maney), 196–197
potential
    empathy and, 67
    high-profile assignments and, 42
    HR and, 120–121
    at Jamba Juice, 38–42
    living up to, 30–31
    organizational, 32–34
    pipeline development for, 105–106
    promotion and hiring based on, 24–26
    underestimating, 30
power, 20
    of business leaders, 2, 174–175
    of culture, 19–20
    of HR, 118
"The Power of Proximity" (Stevenson),
    150–151
privilege
    Amy Cooper incident and, 11–12
    awareness of, 64
    penalized in DEI, 3
proactivity, 84–85, 165
    in dismantling barriers, 99
problem solving, 88–89, 106
professional associations, 64–65, 162–163
profitability, 174–175
Progressive Governance Fund, 178
promotions, 181–182
    action-learning teams and, 139
    based on potential, 24–26
    documenting current practices in, 82–83
    initiatives for, 132–134
    interrupting bias in, 142–144
    for transformation, 78

psychological safety, 123
    bias and emotional tax and, 26
    "left-hand column" for, 111–112
    for speaking freely, 72–73
pulse surveys, 79–80

Quaker Oats, 152–153

racism
    Amy Cooper and, 11–12
    anti-racism and, 172
    business leaders in stopping,
        13–16
    dismantling structural, 115
    interrupting bias and, 134–137
    national conversation about, 180
    resources for understanding, 197
    in seeing potential, 24–26
    systemic, 1–2, 51
    third-degree, 12–13
    unconscious, 12–13
Ralston Purina, 27, 29, 31–32, 108–113
Ramadan, Al, 196–197
real estate industry, 181
recruiting. *See* hiring and recruiting
Rendle, Linda, 102
reputational risk, 158
resilience, 16–22, 159–162, 165
resistance, 9–10, 18–19, 46, 78, 123, 144
resources, 77, 196–201
    for culture audits, 79–80
résumé screening, 121, 182
retention rates, 186–187
Revans, Reginald, 87
Rice, John, 12–13
risk assessment, 165
rituals, 107, 114
Roa, Eric, 156
Rogers, John, 179–180
Rometty, Ginni, 181
Roosevelt, Theodore, 145
Ross University School of Veterinary
    Medicine, 154
roundtable discussions, 71–72, 75
Ruff, Larry, 66–67

Safeway, 38
Sam's Club, 175
Save Our Sons, 23–24
Scharf, Charles, 84
Schnuck, Todd, 23–24, 172
Schnuck Markets, 23–24, 82, 87, 114
Schultz, Howard, 68–69, 123
S-curve framework, 64
Senge, Peter, 109
Services Acquisition Corp., 37
shareholder activism, 178
Sharer, Kevin, 181
Silicon Valley Business Journal, 21
Slootman, Frank, 21
Slubowski, Mike, 184
small wins, 123, 137
Snowflake, 21
social connections, 45–46, 187
social justice, 13–14
social media, 152, 188
social responsibility, 13, 148, 174–175
South Africa, 180
So You Want to Talk about Race (Oluo),
    77, 172
Soy Vay Enterprises, 104
Spencer Stuart, 178
sponsors, 144
Starbucks, 44, 123
    action plan at, 93
    Race Together at, 68–70
STEM talent, 60
Stevens, Matthew, 91, 172
Stevenson, Bryan, 150–151
strategic planning, 37–38, 131
Stretch, Leslie, 59–60, 67, 145, 172
    culture transformation plan of, 95–98
    external resources used by, 77
supply-chain diversity, 22, 147–167
    building, 162–165
    checklist for CEOs on, 166–167
    competitive edge through, 155–162
    economic impact and, 157–158
    reputational risk, 158
    resilience and, 159–162
    risk assessment of, 165
    steps for building, 165–166
sustainability, 99–100, 127–130, 149

sweatshops, 158–159
symbols, 113–114

Tabrizi, Behnam, 128
Target, 13–14, 52–53, 176
    Accelerators, 163
    action plan at, 93
    documentation at, 83–84
    Supplier Diversity Summit, 163
    supply-chain diversity at, 155–157
Target Foundation, 83
task forces, 70, 87–91
Taylor, Breonna, 4
Taylor Bros. Construction Co., 157
teams. *See also* action-learning teams
    (ALTs)
    autonomous, 185
    diversity in, 119–120
technology, 187–189
technology industry, 96
TIAA, 157
Tichy, Noel, 41, 88, 195–196
town halls, 71, 73
Traditional Medicinals, 77
training, 163
    antibias, 69–70
    in bias recognition, 139–140
    empathy, 64–65
    in interrupting bias, 136–137, 140–144
trauma epidemic, 150–151
Trinity Health, 27, 183–185
Trump, Donald, 17, 54, 69–70
Truth and Reconciliation Commission,
    180
Tutu, Desmond, 152
Twilio, 113
Tyson, Bernard, 29, 53–55, 112, 154–155
Tyson Foods, 99

UK Coal Board, 87
United Nations, 188
United States Hispanic Chamber of
    Commerce, 163
University of Missouri, 15–16
US Chamber of Commerce, 179, 181

Index

values, 41
    culture audits and, 79
    dismantling structural bias and, 115–116
    ecosystems and, 148
    empathy, 66–67
    supply chains and, 159
Velez, Alejandro, 191–192
virtual-first culture, 186–187
virtual workplaces, 169–170, 186–187
vision, 18
visual communication, 113–114

Walgreens Boots Alliance, 69, 172, 175–176
The Wall Street Journal, 8–9, 52–53
Walmart, 154
Ward, Laysha, 83
Wardell, Lisa, 56–58, 172
    Covid-19 pandemic and, 153–154
    empathy of, 65–66
    listen-and-learn meetings, 73
    on middle managers, 128–129
    speaking out on bias by, 107–108, 135
Washington, Julie, 27, 32–33, 101–102,
    183–185
wealth gap, 19
Welch, Jack, 88, 104

Wells Fargo, 84
"we working," 185
White, James, 30–31
White, Krista, 3–4, 192–193
White, Rose, 30–31
white supremacist movement, 170
Wilkerson, Isabel, 72, 197
Williams, Joan, 42, 80, 115, 135–136, 140,
    142–143
Williams, Venus, 44, 45
Wilson, Darren, 15, 54
Wingard, Jason, 54–55
Wired magazine, 172–173
Witherspoon, Kamau, 52–53
Women's Business Enterprise National
    Council, 163
Women's Foodservice Forum, 199
work ethic, 30
Workhuman, 118–119
Workplace Experience Survey, 80
workplace of the future, 169–170

XPRIZE Racial Equity Alliance, 199–200

Zara, 158–159

Acknowledgments

The creation of this book could not have happened without the brilliance and support of my family, friends, and colleagues. These acknowledgments cannot contain my immense gratitude to those that made this a possibility. To Jan Alexander, your masterful storytelling, writing, and editing brought this vital work to new heights. To Roger Williams, my exceptional agent and partner, thank you for believing in the work and bringing this project to life. Thanks also to Krista White, brilliant writer, researcher, and my eldest daughter, who inspired me throughout the project.

To Scott Berinato and the team at Harvard Business Review Press, thank you for guiding me through my first book, for your meticulous editing, and for your steadfast support of the vision.

Thank you to my loving family. My wife, Rhonda, played every role—supporter, reviewer, and cheerleader—on the project. Thank you, Rhonda, for your encouragement and for never shying away from constructive criticism. To my youngest daughter, Jasmine, my sister, Cheryl Jones, and my parents, Rose and James White, you are the foundation for all my work. I love you.

To Warner Davis, Bob Roby, Bernard Tyson, Randy Partee, Fritzi Woods, and John Manfredi: Though you are no longer with us, your spirits as incredible leaders, mentors, and friends live on in me and in all that I do. Rest in power!

Acknowledgments

Thank you to the exceptional leaders who participated in the interviews that shaped this book, including Julie Washington, Mike Fuccillo, Janice Duis, Amy Shore, Jackie Reses, Danny Guillory, Lisa Wardell, Leslie Stretch, Erby Foster, Deborah Ashton, PhD, and Lisa Dyson, PhD.

Thank you to Paul Butler, Diane Ashly, Sheryl O'Loughlin, Paul Witkay, and Fred Foulkes for your honest feedback on an early draft of the book.

And thank you to the leaders who coached, mentored, and inspired me, including Joe Bednor, John Kinmonth, Randy Rose, John McGinty, Lin Hart, Glenn Dalton, Trudy Bourgeois, Betsey Cohen, and Polly Dolan.

About the Authors

JAMES D. WHITE is a transformational leader with more than thirty years of experience as a CEO and operating executive. He has overseen the evolution and growth of some of the world's most iconic brands in the consumer products, retail, and restaurant industries. As the former Chair, President, and CEO of Jamba Juice, White led the successful turnaround and transformation of the company from a smoothie shop to a leading global healthy- and active-lifestyle brand, and he has held senior executive roles at Safeway Stores, Gillette, Nestlé Purina PetCare, and Coca-Cola.

A passionate champion for diversity and inclusion, White has been recognized with numerous awards, including the American Heart Association's Corporate Citizen Award and Junior Achievement of Northern California's Lifetime Achievement Award. The *San Francisco Business Times* also named him the San Francisco Bay Area's Most Admired CEO.

White was inducted into the 2021 Alumni Hall of Fame at the University of Missouri. He received an honorary Doctorate of Humane Letters from Fontbonne University and was invited to be the commencement speaker for the class of 2017.

KRISTA WHITE is a writer and consultant in the DEI space, focusing on work at the intersection of race and queerness. She is the founder and CEO of Kiki the App and the cofounder of Culture Design Lab, two DEI-focused startups. An avid traveler and lifelong learner, Krista has studied film at the India Study Abroad Center, writing at the Paris American Academy, user experience design at the General Assembly, and web development at SheCodes. Krista is based in New York City and is a graduate of Columbia University.